Islamic Finance

A PRACTICAL INTRODUCTION

TASNIM NAZEER

THE ISLAMIC FOUNDATION

Islamic Finance: A Practical Introduction

First published in England by
The Islamic Foundation
Markfield Conference Centre, Ratby Lane
Markfield, Leicestershire LE67 9SY, United Kingdom
Email: publications@islamic-foundation.com
Website: www.Islamic-foundation.com

Qur'an House, PO Box 30611, Nairobi, Kenya

PMB 3193, Kano, Nigeria

Distributed by
Kube Publishing Ltd.
Tel: +44(0)1530 249230
e-mail: info@kubepublishing.com

Cataloguing-in-Publication Data is available from the British library

ISBN 978-0-86037-635-4 paperback
ISBN 978-0-86037-658-3 ebook

Cover design and typesetting: Nasir Cadir
Printed by: Mega Basim, Turkey

Contents

Introduction

Islamic Finance as a New Paradigm

Islamic finance and banking is growing at an unprecedented rate around the world, and the impact of the Islamic resurgence has played a pivotal role in shaping the growing success of the industry. The objective of this book is to serve as an introduction to Islamic finance and banking with the aim of providing an invaluable resource that can be utilized by students, professionals and those wishing to learn about Islamic finance from its inception to its future development.

The global financial crisis of July 2007,[1] which was the worst since the Great Depression of the 1930s, played a significant role in highlighting the potential of Islamic finance to an international audience. Many conventional banks and financial institutions were left heavily in debt, due to an economic strategy that had built up increased liquidity and uncertainty in mortgage credit

---

1. H. Alasrag, 'Global Financial Crisis and Islamic Finance', p. 4.

institutions in the United States. In addition, many conventional banks that had been dealing with interest and speculations accumulated an excessive amount of debt which led to an economic spill-over into the international economy.

In September 2008[2] the crisis worsened as the global economy saw a downfall in stock markets, volatile exchange rates and a decrease in international trading. The worldwide economy was affected profoundly, with unemployment at its peak and a drop in industrial production, which further led to a rise in declining incomes and families struggling with financial impediments. Investors, entrepreneurs, businesses, banks, employees and other financial institutions lost out profoundly, which prompted discussion of the foundations of the capitalist financial system.

New ideologies and alternatives to the conventional method of financing were welcomed, and Islamic finance paved the way for a value-based financing that catered for the masses. Islamic economists began to raise awareness of the benefits that Islamic finance contributed in preventing the consequences of another global financial crisis. The Islamic finance industry is therefore seen as a new paradigm that could be used in ethical investment and financial products that can enhance and protect economies worldwide.

An Introduction to the Principles of Islamic Finance

Islamic finance and banking is governed by the tenets of Islam and is based upon the principles of Islamic commercial law. Consequently, the Islamic economic system (as a theoretical framework of Islamic finance) is based upon axioms that construct a code of conduct for Muslims to adhere to when

---

2.   Ibid.

managing their economic activities in an ethical and Shariah compliant manner. Therefore, when understanding the basis of the principles of Islamic finance one has to consider the fact that Muslims believe that economic transactions should take place responsibly, ethically and with the remembrance that Allah (God) is the owner of all wealth. Many non-Muslims find the value-based approach appealing and many have chosen to follow the Islamic financial system when managing their finances.

One of the most important legal aspects of Islamic finance, and one that sets Islamic finance apart from conventional financing, is the absence of *ribā* (interest). *Ribā* is an Arabic word that also means usury, and dealing with *ribā* is a common challenge in the contemporary financial world, which has left many people heavily in debt. Islamic jurisprudence has clearly outlined the complete prohibition of *ribā* when making any financial transactions or deals in a Shariah compliant manner. From an Islamic economic position, *ribā* is considered to create a social injustice due to the fact that in a *ribā*-based transaction, the owner of the wealth obtains profit and the borrower carries all the risk.

This moves on to the next main principle, which is risk sharing, whereby all transactions that are made must be shared by two parties so that both parties have the same level of risk in return for profit. Vice versa, the borrower only pays interest and the owner of the wealth (the creditor) does not share in profit earned by the borrower with the same money. This implies injustice for the weaker party, whether it is debtor or creditor.

Uncertainty, also known as *gharar*, is another distinguishing characteristic of Islamic finance that must be avoided. Both parties must have complete information about the transactions or contracts that they are getting into. A transaction involving gambling, speculation or any prohibited non-Shariah compliant industries, such as alcohol, haram industries and entertainment that does not comply with the fundamental tenets of Shariah, is also to be avoided when making an Islamic financial contract. In addition to fundamental tenets of Islamic commercial law, according to Islamic economics Islamic finance has to consider additional factors, which are presented in Table 1:

Fundamental tenets derived from Shariah	Principle-based (ethics and values)
• Absence of interest-based transactions.	• Principles akin to ethical investing.
• Avoidance of economic activities involving speculation.	• Emphasis on risk sharing and partnership contracts.
• Prohibition on production of goods and services which contradict the values of Islam.	• It is presumed to serve the community, not just the market.
	• Aims to enable and function for individuals.
• Asset-backed transactions with investment in real, durable assets.	• Open to all-faith clients.
• Stability from linking financial services to the productive, real economy.	• Instruments of poverty-reduction are an inherent part of Islamic finance (zakat and *qard al-Ḥasan*).
• Excessive credit and debt products are not encouraged.	
• Restrains consumer indebtedness.	

Table 1: Features of Islamic Financial Contracts

These principles and assigned roles to IBF (Islamic Banking and Finance) are supposed to create a value system beyond normal banking by fulfilling *maqāṣid al-Shariah*, the objectives of Shariah as it has been identified through the values and norms of Islamic economics, which are in contradiction with the pure financialization and profit maximization of conventional finance. However, this aspirational goal has not been accommodated since little of the large amounts of wealth associated with Islamic banking has reached the neediest in Muslim societies. Thus the money in Islamic banks circulates among the large corporate interests in oil rich states. It is therefore no surprise that the emergence of the Islamic banking sector coincides with the oil-shocks and the emergence of oil money in the Gulf in the 1970s.

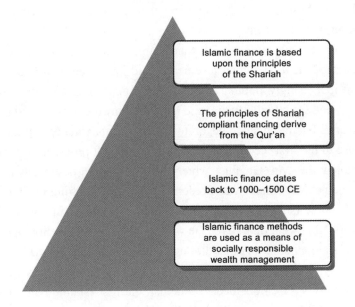

Islamic finance is based
upon the principles
of the Shariah

The principles of Shariah
compliant financing derive
from the Qur'an

Islamic finance dates
back to 1000–1500 CE

Islamic finance methods
are used as a means of
socially responsible
wealth management

Figure 1: Key Points from the Introduction to Islamic Finance

The History of Islamic Finance and Banking

Islamic business models can be dated back to around 1000–1500 CE,[3] when Middle Eastern traders first engaged in Shariah-based transactions between the Middle East and Europe. With the advent of Islam, the Prophet Muhammad (peace be upon him) carried out Shariah-based trading operations for his wife, Khadijah. The tenets of Islamic economic activities were described in the Holy Qur'an in various verses that outlined the economic system through which transactions have to take place. Middle Eastern traders often referred back to these principles when dealing with

3.   N. Schoon, 'Islamic Finance - a History', p. 10.

Islamic business transactions and adhered to risk-sharing without interest and *gharar*.

It was only in the 1970s that Islamic finance and banking in its modern form began to emerge, and has since then become an increasingly popular way of financing, which has received demand from both Muslim and non-Muslim countries around the world. Islamic finance began to flourish exponentially and gave rise to the first recognizable Shariah compliant project in Egypt, called the Mit Ghamr,[4] which was a Shariah-based savings scheme. Mit Ghamr was predominantly a risk-sharing business. The first Islamic banking model was introduced in Egypt in 1963[5] and went on to pave the way for subsequent developments of Islamic banks and institutions in the developing countries.

By 1975,[6] the Finance Ministers at the Organization of Islamic Countries (OIC) decided to establish the first Islamic bank, the Islamic Development Bank (IDB). The fundamental goal of the bank was to enhance developmental needs by providing financial assistance and support for OIC countries based on the principles of Shariah. The main aims of the IDB were to be an established international financial institution that aided in nurturing Islamic finance services and fostered development of the industry in a Shariah compliant manner. The IDB was unprecedented in being the very first international financial institution to run its financial services in a Shariah compliant way. There are currently fifty-six countries[7] that are members of the IDB and OIC and the bank has evolved significantly following the rise in demand for Islamic finance around the world.

---

4.   Ibid., p. 11.
5.   F. Hadžić, 'Conventional and Islamic Banking', pp. 14.
6.   A. Ahmad, 'Evolution of Islamic Banking', p. 339.
7.   L. Dean, 'Islamic Development Bank', p. 1328.

Since the establishment of the IDB, there have been many Islamic financial institutions and conventional banks set up around the world aiming to cater to the demand for Shariah compliant services. Many mainstream banks, such as HSBC, have set up Islamic windows to offer Islamic financial services to customers who wish to conduct their finances according to the principles of Islam. The Islamic banking industry was further spurred through the IDB, as it was the first time that an international financial institution was in support of conforming their financial services in adherence to the principles of the Shariah.

The fact that the Islamic finance and banking industry is growing at an unprecedented rate is due to historical factors that have paved the way for the sector to develop. Historically, conventional commercial banking could not easily offer funds to industrialists, entrepreneurs, traders and manufacturers without the interest-based system. There was no clear alternative to the commercial banking sector in the post-colonial period of Muslim countries, even though the principles of Islamic finance were set in place as early as the times of the Prophet Muhammad (peace be upon him).

After the independence of Muslim countries and the failure of their economic development, the 1970s was a key period for the Islamic financial industry to emerge. However, due to the industrial revolution, many companies sought to obtain funds from conventional institutions, as there were not enough sources to fund their own companies without the use of commercial borrowing. Financial intermediation, which was much sought after by companies in the 1970s, was the main reason for the success of a type of commercial banking that left ethical and religious considerations behind. As a result of the impending industrialization, Muslim borrowers who wanted to follow Islamic principles in the commercial world were left with little choice, unless there was the development of an Islamic financial institution that would meet the needs of managing their finances. The western banking sector had begun to promote commercial banking as opposed to social financing and was not grabbing the interest of the Muslim world. This brought about a realization of the need for interest-free banking as an ethical method of financing that is based on a smooth flowing banking system.

The Muslim countries began developing Islamic banking institutions that aimed to cater for small businesses and provide assistance to businesses that did not want to use commercial banking. Nasser Islamic Bank was developed in 1971[8] and began operating a year later with the purpose of providing interest free loans that was based on a profit sharing system. In 1975, Dubai Islamic Bank began operating its services for interest free Islamic banking and by the 1980s more Islamic financial banking institutions were being set up, such as Al Bakarah group in the Gulf. Many Muslim countries, such as Malaysia, Iran, and Bangladesh, established Islamic banking sectors and set up their own Islamic banks with support from their governments. In addition, non-Muslim countries responding to the needs of Muslim investors, such as the Philippines, Denmark and Luxembourg, also began to tap into models of Islamic finance and establish Islamic banks.

In the twenty-first century there has been an increase in demand for Islamic banking, with the establishment of many Islamic banks and windows in major western countries such as the UK. This rise was due to the global economic crisis that left many businesses and banks heavily in debt. The crisis, which mainly affected the western world's commercial banking sector, businesses and entrepreneurs, highlighted the flaws of the conventional banking system. The Islamic finance system was brought into the spotlight and many investors and entrepreneurs,

---

8.   Ahmad, 'Evolution of Islamic Banking', p. 354.

who had lost out on conventional banking investments, now started to recognize Islamic finance as a new possible alternative. The Islamic finance and banking industry was noted as having many benefits in comparison to the commercial banking system, primarily because it is based on a strict no interest policy. There could not have been a better time for Islamic banks and institutions to develop, as many people began desperately looking for alternatives to commercial banking in order to avoid another economic downfall. Many investors began looking into the advantages of ethical-based investments and financial methods that avoided the use of interest and speculation. Undoubtedly, the global economic crisis which shook the world played a pivotal role in arousing awareness of the Islamic finance and banking industry. The crisis had also raised concerns regarding the conventional financial system and capitalist methods of managing the economy that had taken rise around the world, through predominantly interest and speculative-based products, in banks and financial institutions.

The innovation of Islamic finance and banking provided people with an alternative to managing their finances with risk sharing models in comparison to conventional modes of financing. Due to the ethical principles of Islamic finance, both Muslims and non-Muslims found Islamic financial products and services appealing. Muslims wishing to utilize Shariah compliant finance in adherence to their faith, and non-Muslims who also wanted to manage their finances in a socially responsible manner, began seeking out global Islamic financial institutions. This opened up the scope for the development of fully-fledged Islamic banks and Islamic windows, which began to emerge in conventional banks to cater for the growing demand.

Major Islamic financial hubs were prospering, and international financial centres such as the United Kingdom began to see a rise in opportunities to offer Shariah compliant banking services. Al Rayan Bank (previously the Islamic Bank of Britain) was established in early 2004 and is the UK's first ever fully-fledged Islamic retail bank. The UK also issued the very first Islamic bond (ṣukūk), which was a major first for the country to establish itself as an Islamic financial centre in the west. Many western countries are tapping into the potential of the increasingly popular Islamic finance industry and are hoping to be major players as Islamic financial hubs that cater for Islamic financing.

There are many countries that are prospering as notable Islamic financial hubs and continue to develop new standards, products, services and opportunities for investors, entrepreneurs and customers. Some of the major Islamic financial hubs to date include countries such as Malaysia, Indonesia, Pakistan, Iran, Turkey, Dubai, Abu Dhabi, Qatar, Bahrain and Saudi Arabia. With the population of Muslims growing around the world there is unprecedented scope for the offering of Shariah compliant products and services that are not merely confined to the Arab world alone, but are also appealing to the west.

The historical events that played a crucial impact on the financial world, such as the global economic crisis, have helped to further highlight the advantages of Islamic finance and banking in comparison to conventional banking. Although conventional banking and the capitalist financial system dominate much of today's financial management, there is scope for Islamic finance to become a strong competitor to the conventional financial services industry.

The expansion of Islamic finance investments worldwide and various establishments of Islamic banks and windows are catering for the demand for ethical financing. The historical progression of the Islamic finance industry has paved the way for the industry to evolve on a global scale and further prosper in the years to come.

Shariah Law

Modern Islamic finance and banking is based upon Shariah law, which is central to a Muslim's regulation and conduct of how best to manage their finances and banking needs. Shariah law plays a crucial role in outlining the principles of managing finance in an Islamic manner and provides the benchmark for Muslims to follow from the Qur'an and Prophet Muhammad's teachings. Shariah law clearly differentiates Islamic finance and banking from conventional finance. This is due to the fact that the Islamic financial system is based upon the codes of conduct outlined by the Shariah and promotes a set of core values that provide a distinguished way of managing wealth.

One of the key elements of Islamic finance is that any amount of money has no intrinsic value. A Muslim cannot borrow or receive money with interest according to the laws of Islamic finance. The wealth that is accumulated in a Shariah compliant manner can only be invested through legitimate investments of assets and trade that complies with Islamic law. In addition, uncertainty of a transaction or investment, also known as *gharar*, is prohibited. Islamic finance also prohibits investment in products and industries which are socially irresponsible and go against the tenets of Islam such as alcohol, pornography, tobacco, prostitution, pork or any other product based on gambling and immoral services.

Islamic finance and banking that complies with the Shariah, is predominantly based on trading, and all activities of Shariah compliant trading have to have the element of risk sharing. The principle of profit-and-loss sharing (PLS) is an essential axis of the IBF, around which economic and business activities take place. This considers ways to prevent the capital owner from shifting the entire risk onto the borrower, and hence it aims at establishing justice between work effort and return, and between work effort and capital. As a consequence, this feature of IBF requires offering a participatory nature of economic and business activity between shareholders and stakeholders through Islamic financial constructs (*muḍārabah*, *mushārakah*).

Many Islamic banking and finance institutions around the world refer to experts in the field of Shariah law to ensure that all products and services offered comply with the fundamental tenets of Shariah. There are various supervisory committees and scholars that authorize Islamic financial products and services to fully-fledged Islamic institutions and those wishing to open Islamic finance windows at conventional banks. Many financial governing bodies and authorities of Islamic finance institutions and banks have scholars and experts in place to seek guidance from and to help in giving a ruling on whether a transaction, product or service is legitimately compliant with the Shariah.

Shariah law is the code of conduct that affects all aspects of a Muslim's life, and it regulates several restrictions when it comes to managing finances in an Islamic manner. The two most significant effects of Shariah law on Islamic banking and financial transactions are the prohibition of interest and dealing with impermissible haram investments. Shariah law provides the framework for all aspects of Islamic investments, transactions and project deals and continues to play an important role in the authorization and compliance of Islamic products and services around the world.

Regulation in Islamic Finance

The regulatory system of Islamic finance that governs Shariah compliant financial institutions varies significantly across countries, although there has been a demand for standardization of the industry on the global level. The growing number of

Islamic financial institutions and windows that have opened in various countries has further spurred the need for a harmonized method of regulating the Islamic finance and banking industry. Standardization of regulating a growing industry is invaluable in seeking the growth of the industry and helps to create a benchmark for institutions to seek and follow guidance.

A number of international organizations have been established in order to set standards that would strengthen and eventually harmonize regulations for Islamic financial investments, transactions, products and services, and there are a number of key regulatory authorities that govern the industry. The Islamic Financial Services Board (IFSB) was set up in 2002 to provide an international regulatory body made up of standard setting agents to provide benchmark and supervisory guidelines for Islamic financial institutions around the world. The IFSB aids in regulating Islamic banks, capital markets and insurance and highlights the development of a transparent Islamic finance and banking industry, and also aims to introduce new standards and cater for international standards that are compliant with the principles of the Shariah. The IFSB complements the work of the Basel Committee and is based in the Islamic financial hub of Kuala Lumpur, Malaysia.

Islamic finance and banking requires global Shariah compliant regulators to evaluate related risks and benefits. Despite the fact that Islamic banks offer profit-and-loss sharing accounts and therefore expose limited risk of insolvency, there is still the existence of potential systemic risks that need to be looked into by an authoritative body. The international Basel Accords, which are the standards of regulating international banks worldwide that all banks have to adhere to, does not include Islamic banks. However, the new systems of Basel II and III credit risk rating has introduced more compatibility for Islamic banking. In order to maintain financial stability in Islamic financial institutions and control any risks, regulators have needed to ensure that Islamic banks should adopt international regulations such as Basel II and III. Such regulation aid in supporting Islamic banks to be able to compete internationally and be exposed to the benefits of compatibility. Due to the nature of Islamic finance and banking, which prohibits the use of interest and uncertainty, the regulatory system poses significant differences in comparison to the regulation of a conventional bank or financial institution.

There are a number of significant challenges of regulating the Islamic financial system, due to factors such as capital adequacy, knowledge of the Shariah and standardization on the rulings of a fatwa, which determine whether a product, investment or transaction is legitimately Shariah compliant. Islamic banks and financial institutions operate with unique products and services that do not comply with conventional banks or financial institutions. For this reason, unique Islamic financial products may carry risks, which need regulating and require risk measurement and effective capital adequacy measures. In addition, the lack of experts in Islamic financial regulation can pose a challenge to determining Shariah compliancy.

Although there are challenges in the regulation of Islamic finance and banking there have been many positive developments, which are paving the way for a standardized regulatory system which can harmonize the industry. The presence of organizations such as the Accounting and Auditing Organisation for Islamic Financial Institutions (AAOIFI) has helped to strengthen the regulation of the growing industry worldwide. The AAOIFI acts as an international Islamic non-profit corporate body that specializes in the accounts, auditing, governance, ethics and standards of Shariah for Islamic financial institutions and the Islamic banking industry. The AAOIFI has garnered support from over two hundred institutional members from over forty countries deriving from central banks, Islamic financial institutions and the international Islamic banking and financial industry that are prevalent worldwide.[9] As of 2018 there are a total of 100[10] standards, forty-eight standards are based upon the Shariah, twenty-six on accounting, five on auditing, seven on governance and two on the codes of ethics. These standards for regulating the Islamic financial industry have been implemented by various countries worldwide and many countries have voluntarily based their financial guidelines for Sharia compliant finance on AAOIFI's standards.

Another notable regulatory and standard setting authority for the Islamic finance and banking industry is the International Islamic Financial Market (IIFM). Focusing on aiding the standardization of the Islamic finance industry worldwide and catering for setting standards, the IIFM is predominantly focused on Islamic capital and markets. The IIFM works collectively to provide global standardized Islamic financial documentation of Islamic finance products and services and helps to create unification of the increasingly growing industry worldwide. The IIFM works with Shariah advisory panels that include renowned scholars, which provide assurance to those wishing to determine Shariah compliancy when managing their finances. The challenges of standardization of regulation of the industry can often pose a threat to the development of the industry globally, as those wishing to manage their finances ethically do not want to be misled.

The new standards, which are being developed progressively by authoritative regulatory bodies of Islamic finance, can aid in dispelling any potential confusion when determining the authenticity of a Shariah compliant financial product or service.

---

9. 'About AAOIFI' (AAOIFI; Accounting and Auditing Organisation for Islamic Financial Institutions, undated).
10. Ibid.

Due to the establishment of organizations such as the IIFM, AAOIFI and IFSB and other regulatory authorities worldwide for Islamic finance and banking, there is more scope for harmonization of the Islamic finance industry.

CHAPTER 1

Key Principles Governing Islamic Finance

Islamic finance is based upon adherence to the principles of the Shariah, which determines the codes of conduct for Muslims to adhere to in order to follow an Islamic way of life. Principles of Shariah law affect the economic, political and social conduct pertaining to Muslims and helps followers establish the right balance in managing all aspects of their life in a responsible and well informed manner. Some of the core underlying spiritual values of Islamic economics include the acknowledgement that Allah is the giver and owner of all wealth. Muslims believe that they have been entrusted with the wealth they have acquired and understand that they are fully responsible for the way they use their earnings and investments, which should be utilized according to that expectation of trust (*amānah*).

One of the significant differences between conventional finance and Islamic finance is the fact that Islamic finance is based upon a no-interest policy and interest is strictly prohibited in all financial deals, transactions or investments.

Ribā (interest) is prohibited because it can result in societal injustice that would go against the tenets of Islam. In a *ribā*-based transaction, the owner of the wealth gets a return without making any effort, and the borrower carries all the risk, which means that the principle of risk sharing is neglected and therefore would not be accepted as a Shariah compliant method of managing finance.

The principles underlying Islamic behaviour are not only ethical but are also spiritually based. A Muslim's economic activities and the way that an individual manages their wealth should contain a balance with the spiritual aspects of their life. The fundamental principles of Islamic finance are based upon the Shariah. If an individual manages their finances in adherence to the Shariah it is considered to be an act of worship, and this shows the importance and influence that Islam plays in all aspects of life, including managing finances.

In Islamic finance, any economic transaction should take place within justified and responsible economic expectations by essentializing *maqāṣid al-Shariah* (objectives of Islamic law). The principles of Islam outline the best ways to conduct economic activities and promote the concept of financial responsibility and sustainability when dealing with other people. Islam enables individuals to deal with their finances in a free-market environment and economy where the supply and demand are decided in the market itself. However, the function of the market is imposed by principles of Shariah articulated within the concept of *hisbah* (the market regulations and supervisions).

The main purpose for imposing the laws and ethics for fulfilling *maqāṣid al-Shariah* is in order to promote moral and social justice when dealing with finance. This means that the wealth earned by any individual is not profited only by a few investors or businesses whilst leaving others to suffer. According to Islamic law, risk should be carried equally between the two and this provides a highly ethical and socially responsible method of managing finance.

The fundamental principles of Islamic finance will be discussed individually in this chapter in detail. There are a few core principles that are compulsory to be applied in Islamic finance and banking and these are the sharing of profit, loss and risks, the prohibition of *ribā*, prohibition of uncertainty in transactions, the existence of an underlying asset and adherence to purely Shariah compliant investments and not those that deal with immoral industries such as pork, alcohol, pornography, gambling or any other prohibited investment.

The prohibition of interest is significant as an underlying principle, which provides a philosophy – or model – which helps to fulfil the other principles that govern Islamic finance in order to establish the wider objectives in the area of business. The fundamental principles of Islamic finance and banking also involve the acknowledgement of developmental and social economic goals as essentialized by Islamic developmentalism (*'imrān*). The profit, loss and risk sharing element enables finance to be conducted justly and is believed to hold more economic benefits than conventional methods of profit sharing. *Ribā* is often seen as unfair gain or exploitation of money and one that is often used in a capitalist system.

Transactions that are reliant upon a matter of chance and leave room for speculation rather than a joint effort from both investors to produce a return, are considered invalid under the Shariah. The principles of Shariah do not extend to the prohibition of commercial speculation or risk taking, as transactions involving the use of options must be carefully checked for legitimacy as to whether the transaction is adherent to the Shariah. The presence of ambiguity in any transaction, also known as *gharar*, is not allowed when making any investment or financial deal. This complies with the principle that all transactions should be transparent and the various parties involved must present a full disclosure. Any type of transaction that fails to have full trust and transparency from both parties becomes invalid under Shariah law.

The principle of the prohibition of investing in impermissible industries such as pork, alcohol, pornography, gambling, conventional finance or any other industry which goes against the tenets of Islam is highly significant in Islamic finance. Islamic finance promotes an ethical system that aims to facilitate an honourable living based on financing that aims to benefit the society at large. Conventional financing does not take into account whether the investments are ethical or the impact of certain investments on society, such as investing in products that could potentially cause harm to the community. Islamic finance, however, provides a system whereby the impact of how money is spent is carefully considered from the onset. It offers an individual the opportunity to create and use their wealth responsibly, while following a system not created by human rulers but by divine guidance.

The principles of Islamic finance form the basis for all investments, transactions, products and services and provide a benchmark for Islamic financial institutions to turn to in conducting their business. All Islamic financial institutions have to abide by the laws outlined in the Islamic commercial law in conducting their businesses and product offerings. The main difference between conventional methods of financing and Islamic finance is based upon the fact that Islamic finance offers individuals a system and benchmark of ethical principles to refer to when conducting their finances. These principles are not merely a set of rules but are an important part of a Muslim's adherence to their faith, and hold both spiritual significance as well as an economically ethical approach to handling finance. All Islamic banks and financial institutions that offer Islamic-based financial products have to refer to the principles of the Shariah and are authenticated by the authority of Shariah boards or scholars. Shariah supervisory boards are often used to determine whether a potential Islamic financial product is deemed as legitimately Shariah compliant or not. The basis for the fatwa (opinion) given to Islamic financial institutions as to whether a product is compliant or not, is based upon the adherence to the principles of Islamic finance as outlined in Figure 1.1.

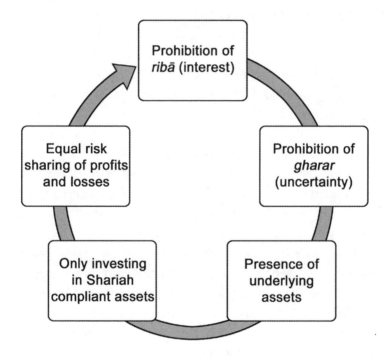

Figure 1.1: A Review of the Key Principles of Islamic Finance

1.1 *Ribā*

Ribā is the Arabic term used in the Qur'an that means interest or usury, and it is strictly prohibited in adherence to Shariah compliant finance. The term *ribā* also refers to the increase or profit made by a lender who gains excess profits with no effort. This is because the role of *ribā* is to be a loan for the borrower, who will have to pay compensation or more profit to the lender than the actual amount that he or she initially borrowed. Islam considers interest to be unjust and immoral and the avoidance of interest is reiterated in the Holy Qur'an in many verses such as:

> *O you who believe! Fear Allah, and give up what remains of your demand for usury, if ye are indeed believers.*
> (*al-Baqarah* 2: 278)

There are various verses in the Qur'an that outline the importance of dealing justly when managing finances and strictly forbids the use of interest in any transaction or dealing. The predetermined price of capital which a lender states in an interest-based transaction is clearly prohibited, as the principle amount borrowed has to be protected under the laws of the Shariah and any excess profits made will be deemed as exploitative and unjust. In accordance with Islamic commercial law, any form of *ribā*-based transaction is a major sin for a Muslim and gaining unjustly through trade, business or investments, which gain excess profit with no effort, is considered exploiting the borrower.

There are two main types of *ribā* which are discussed by Islamic jurists: an increase in capital without any services provided and speculation, which is prohibited by the Qur'an, and commodity exchanges in unequal quantities, which are also prohibited in accordance with the ethical principles outlined in adherence to the Holy Qur'an. As the Qur'an is an undisputed light of guidance for all Muslims, all scholars and Muslim authorities agree unanimously that *ribā* is explicitly forbidden and any transaction or investment involving usurious activities would not be considered to be adhering to the Qur'an or Sunnah. According to the principles of Islamic commercial law, *ribā* is a form of oppression and a means to unjustly take an increase of money from others with no effort. *Ribā* has been deemed as exploiting a borrower's needs and circumstances with the lender unjustly progressing in profit. Islam, therefore, forbids a *ribā*-based system altogether and promotes the giving of charity as a highly ethical and beneficial alternative.

One of the main differences between Islamic finance and its conventional counterpart is that it provides a highly ethical approach to financing which deals with individuals justly and provides them with an alternative to being exploited through paying in excess. The global economic crisis left many people heavily in debt, including conventional banks, entrepreneurs and investors who had used the capitalist interest-based system and were unable to pay back the excess amount of interest that they had on their loans. Islamic finance protects the payment of an individual and enables them to benefit from not having to pay a surplus charge when borrowing money from an individual or institution.

There are many challenges that conventional financial institutions and banks have when dealing with *ribā* and there are many benefits to the ethical non-interest based financing that Islamic finance promotes and provides. *Ribā* is the income earned by the borrowed financial capital despite there being no effort from the lender, so the risk is carried completely by the borrower of the loan. The capital owner is considered as exploiting the borrower because any excess profit is gained through undeserved income achieved without producing or offering anything and without contributing any value to the revenue. The mechanism

Not Entirely Point.
but I get the Point

of a *ribā*-based system that conventional banks and financial institutions use has prevented the distribution of economic activities between the lender and borrower and subsequently worsens the distribution of income. The capital owner gains a certain and fixed percentage of earnings in any case, regardless of the gains of a considerable higher capital, which can leave the borrower heavily in debt and is considered to be an oppressive form of financing.

The main rationale for the prohibition of *ribā*, in accordance to the principles of Shariah, is that it is oppression involving exploitation of an excess capital gained by the lender with all risks being left on the borrower. The explicit exclusion of *ribā* ensures that Islamic finance is a justified and ethical way of managing finances and gaining its due share when dealing with transactions, projects or investments.

1.2 Profit and Risk Sharing

Profit and risk sharing of any investment or transaction holds great significance in Islamic finance. All profits and risks are to be shared equally among the parties involved so that one side does not carry the burden of a higher risk than the other. This provides an ethical and just method of managing the risks involved when participating in an investment, project or transaction. The importance of profit and risk sharing in Islamic finance and banking cannot be understated.

Profit-and-loss sharing (PLS) is a form of a partnership between two parties or more and is believed to hold more economic benefits than conventional, collateral-based lending, which favours only well established businesses. The principle of sharing profits and losses equally acknowledges the fact that profits cannot always be assured. In this case, an Islamic financial institution must ensure that they carry part of the risk of a given transaction. There should be no assumption of a guarantee of a fixed return when dealing with a profit-and-loss sharing transaction, which means that both depositors and Islamic financial institutions cannot invest under the impression that they will gain a guaranteed return. Seeking protection or a method of security is allowed in a PLS contract in order to safeguard against any breach of the contract by either party.

Raising funds through PLS according to the principles of Shariah has a number of benefits over conventional interest linked borrowing. Both entrepreneurs and society can reap the advantages of risk sharing as an alternative to conventional loans, which are considered to be far more risky to issuers than raising funds by way of risk sharing securities. Issuers of risk sharing securities are not required to provide investors with predetermined profits or capital guarantees. This is one of the major advantages of financing in accordance to the principles of the Shariah. The principle of PLS can also enhance the stability of financial institutions, as the sharing of risks can significantly reduce the risk facing any single party so one side does not become overburdened with debt. Utilizing PLS as part of Shariah compliant financing can also be more conducive to economic growth than financing by accumulating debt or being responsible for owing money to a financial institution. Since funds raised through risk sharing are not returned to investors, they continue to remain in the pool of income.

Another advantage of risk sharing, according to the principles of Islamic finance, is it helps to distribute wealth and profits more evenly, as more people can share the profits of a successful business or investment. A wider and transparent distribution of wealth can arouse many benefits for all parties involved. There are two main types of PLS contracts that are used in Islamic finance, such as *mushārakah* and *muḍārabah* contracts, which can be utilized for short, medium and long-term financing agreements for a Shariah compliant project or investment. The mechanism of a profit-and-loss sharing principle that is utilized in all Islamic finance transactions can help to spur the economy forward in a just and ethical way.

In short, PLS contracts in Islamic finance are praised for providing distinguishing features of Islamic financial products (*mushārakah* and *muḍārabah*) but their overall presence is insignificant within IBF institutions. Favouring debt-based products has been justified because of the issue of risk which is associated with PLS contracts and the failure of IBF to provide suitable products for their customers. Generally, banks are inclined to negotiate a profit rate on their saving deposits with potential investors, but on the other hand, when a customer requests borrowing funds, banks are very strict and in many cases customers will not achieve the strict matrix of qualifying for a loan.

More volatile & lot more complex ? The role of the financier becomes much more complex.

1.3 Exclusion of Forbidden Assets

Islamic finance is based upon the principles of Islamic commercial law, which exclude any type of investment in impermissible or forbidden assets, and relies upon solely investing in the real economy, beyond synthetic financing. An investment in the industry sectors of alcohol, gambling, interest, pornography, prostitution, uncertainty or any other industry that does not adhere to the tenets of Islam is strictly forbidden. This is because Islamic finance is reliant upon being socially responsible, and an individual is therefore encouraged to invest in ethical and charitable projects that can better society at large. Shariah compliant financing excludes investments in products or industries that it considers to be harmful to society and a threat to social responsibility, and this is taken very seriously when constituting what is deemed to be a legitimate Shariah compliant investment.

In modern intermediation of Islamic financial institutions, it is an obligation of the investor to ensure that what they are investing in is beneficial and wholesome to society. All investors have to ensure that investments adhere to the principles of the Shariah and comply with the tenets of Islam when investing their wealth. It is for this reason that Islamic financial investments should be made with consideration of the business, values, policies and the products or services that it provides. Among the facets of the Islamic financial system are specific regulations in line with the principles of the Shariah that guide investors in how they should manage their finances. An example of this is in the securities and trading market; an investor may want to consider the company that they are potentially getting involved with and its activities to ensure that it adheres to the principles of investment in real assets.

The benefits of making pure and responsible investments in a business, project or enterprise is believed to reap rewards in comparison to conventional financing, which allows you to indulge in unethical investments of any kind. Some conventional investment industries may be immoral or exploitative to members of society. The tenets of Islamic finance therefore protect society by providing guidelines on what is a deemed a Shariah compliant investment and what is considered a harmful investment. Investments in real economy, such as agriculture, manufacturing, trade, infrastructure and education, adhere to the principles of the Shariah and are encouraged as they are deemed to be prosperous industries for benefitting the society at large.

Shariah compliancy and a consideration of the ethical and social aspects of investing is a key component of Islamic financial investments. Investing in permissible industries plays a crucial impact in the promotion of ethics of Islamic business law. There are many scholars and Shariah supervisory boards that pass fatwas on investment projects, products and potential services to authorize whether they comply with the Shariah or not. Islamic supervisory boards and authorities can help in passing judgments regarding whether an investment is legitimate under the principles of Islamic commercial law. Islam only excludes investments in assets which are considered to be harmful to the society at large or unethical and immoral, and this can only help to promote and increase the rise of beneficial projects around the world.

1.4 Existence of an Asset-Based Transaction

Islamic finance and banking is reliant upon an underlying asset-based transaction in all dealings. The existence of an asset-based transaction must involve real assets that adhere to the principles of the Islamic law. All Shariah compliant sales transactions must be conducted on a real asset value, and the asset must exist, except in *salam* (a sale in which the price is paid at once for goods to be delivered later) and *istiṣnā'* (a contract of manufacture), and be fully owned by the seller. This ensures that the transaction which is being carried out, or the investment of a project, is based upon the sale of a real asset for a specific sum of money.

All Islamic financial transactions must be of the exchange of a commodity or asset for money or commodity. There are a few specific Shariah-based financial contracts that can facilitate legitimate sale transactions, such as *murābaḥah*, *mushārakah*, *ijārah* and *salam*. The existence of an underlying asset means that a buyer of any commodity can purchase an asset with cash, credit or through a financial intermediary. When a financial intermediary is used they must ensure that they fully purchase the asset before selling it on to the buyer in order to ensure that the transaction made is completely Shariah compliant. In acquiring the asset, the financier must also ensure that the commodity is permissible in accordance with the principles of Islamic finance. This assurance will prevent the occurrence of prohibited elements in the transactions. According to the principles of Islamic finance, the role of money in a transaction must be utilized as a medium of exchange only and other commodities determine its sole value. Therefore, unlike conventional financing and interest-backed assets, Islamic asset-based transactions do not consider trading money as a commodity but consider the need for real assets as part of an exchange to be conducted between the two parties.

1.5 *Gharar* and *Maysir*: Uncertainty and Gambling Transactions

A significant principle that underlies all Islamic financial transactions or investments is the prohibition of uncertainty when making an investment or business deal in compliance with the Shariah. *Gharar* is the Arabic term for uncertainty and occurs in instances when there is a contract which is not transparent between the two parties involved. The prohibition of *gharar* ensures there is no conflict or ambiguity at any stage and that all profits from an investment and any losses accumulated will be eventually apportioned in order to avoid uncertainty on the returns on the profits or investment between the investors.

Gharar also constitutes the ambiguity or unnecessary risk of a transaction and can occur when contracted goods or services are inadequately specified; the price of a product may be unknown; or payment terms are uncertain in deferred sales. *Gharar* also refers to the uncertainty of a contract due to lack of disclosure and deliberate avoidance of transparency, which could have been avoided by simply adding more information to the contract.

Selling goods without a proper description, or promising a sale of products that you are unable to deliver, also constitute *gharar* and it is strictly forbidden to mislead a party according to the ethical principles of Islamic finance. This is why most derivative contracts, which are short selling, are forbidden and considered invalid according to the principles of the Shariah because of the uncertainty involved in the future delivery of the underlying asset. Full disclosure and transparency between the sales of goods in trade in accordance with Islamic commercial law can help to protect and prevent against any unexpected losses and possible disagreements between the parties involved in the sale and receipt of goods.

Maysir is the Arabic term for speculation or a gambling transaction, and it is believed that both *gharar* and *maysir* are closely related – as where there is uncertainty it is always a gamble and risk. An example of *maysir* is an insurance contract when a policyholder contributes a premium amount in order to obtain an increase in the sum of money. This is risky because the policyholder may lose the money that they initially paid for the premium when the event that has been insured for does not happen. This is considered unfair and unethical according to the principles of the Shariah, which is one of the reasons why gambling transactions and uncertainty is excluded from Shariah compliant financing.

An example of *maysir* is investing wealth in a casino, playing the lottery, gambling or betting on the races, and any other activity where there is a risk of a total loss or complete gain for one party alone. There are considerable risks involved in speculative transactions, such as the fact that an individual can lose everything and become bankrupt through gambling. In addition, some individuals could become addicted to gambling or taking risks, which may have dire consequences and leave them heavily in debt. Therefore, the ethical principles of Islamic finance prevent individuals from indulging in harmful activities involving their wealth in order to protect the individual from further societal harm.

In conclusion, prohibiting interest, uncertainty (*gharar*), speculation and gambling is justified with the same rationale of emphasizing asset-based productive economic activity. However, new legal (*fiqhi*) scholarship is willing to facilitate acceptable levels of uncertainty for development of modern Islamic financial instruments.

Broadly :

» Focus on underlying asset

» Profit & Loss Sharing.

⮡ But note that P&S requires a lot more complexity -

↠ Note as well that _Enforcement_ of salams etc can be considerably more difficult.

✦ Overall ⟶ The Financial institution just needs to wear alot more hats.

CHAPTER 2

Islamic Banking

Islamic banking is growing at an unprecedented rate around the world and is rapidly becoming an increasingly popular alternative to conventional banking. This is mainly because by following Shariah rulings provides an additional level of security for investors. Many fully-fledged Islamic banks have been set up in Islamic financial hubs of the Muslim world, western countries and non-conventional financial centres, which have recognized the potential in offering Shariah compliant banking products and services to cater for the rising demand.

In the process of developing and creating its market position, IBF was driven by customer demand for more diversified products, such as student loans, mortgages, hedging contracts, Islamic bonds, etc., but at the same time was differentiated from conventional banking, resulting in replication of most conventional products. The process required application of several traditional Islamic concepts in order to create a similar conventional contract, which once developed became less efficient and more complicated and expensive.

The ethical approach of Islamic banking provides a religiously acceptable method of financing for Muslims wishing to manage their finances according to the Islamic faith. This is a sound basis for the system of Islamic banking and all procedures; transactions, products and services that run in an Islamic bank have to be wholly Shariah compliant in order for them to be considered legitimate.

Islamic banking is reliant upon the foundational axioms of Islamic economics and legal principles of Islamic commercial law, which all Islamic banks are supposed to implement in the operations of their bank when offering products and services to customers. The ideas of interest-free Islamic banking on the basis of a profit sharing scheme as an alternative to using *ribā* were first noted in the early financial literary works of Anwar Qureshi (1946), Naiem Siddiqi (1948) and Mahmud Ahmad (1952).[1] All three authors recognized that the implications of dealing with *ribā* went against the tenets of Islamic banking and highlighted the potential of a banking system based on the *muḍārabah* Islamic contract, which promotes a system of sharing risks of profit-and-loss.

In the early 1970s,[2] the research and development of an interest-free bank that complies with Islamic principles began to see progress with financial institutional involvement. The 1970s saw the conference of the Finance Ministers of the Islamic Countries held in Karachi, Pakistan, the Egyptian study in 1972, the First International Conference on Islamic Economics in Saudi Arabia in 1976 and the International Economic Conference in London in 1977 discussing the issue of no-interest banking in compliance with the Shariah. The discussion surrounding the principles of Islamic banking saw more progress as both financial institutions and governments proceeded in the establishment of

1. A. Gafoor, *Interest Free Commercial Banking*, p. 219.
2. Ibid.

the first Shariah compliant banks, which promoted interest-free banking. The establishment of interest-free banking saw the unprecedented development of the Islamic Development Bank in 1975[3] and the very first privately-owned Shariah compliant bank was established in the UAE; the Dubai Islamic Bank was established by a group of Muslim businessmen from several countries in 1975.[4] The growth of Islamic banks and financial institutions began to accelerate as two more private Shariah compliant banks were set up in 1977 – the Faisal Islamic Bank in Egypt and Sudan and the Kuwait Finance House.

Since the inception of these early Islamic banks there has been an unprecedented growth in popularity for their services. Dubai Islamic Bank and Kuwait Finance House are both leading players in the Islamic financial market of today and continue to offer Shariah compliant services to their customers. The implementation of the first ever fully-fledged Al Rayan Bank (previously Islamic Bank of Britain) was a milestone for a European country and a financial centre such as Britain, to establish a bank that offered wholly Islamic financial products and services to its customers. In addition, more western countries around the world also recognized the benefits of Islamic banking in comparison to conventional banking methods.

Islamic windows have been tried and tested in many mainstream conventional banks, such as HSBC Amanah in the United Kingdom, but there are challenges when offering Shariah compliant service windows in conventional banks due to the fact that the main services in conventional banks do not follow the principles of no interest. Offering services which are Shariah compliant to customers from conventional banks may not garner trust to the legitimacy of the products or services. This may result

---

3. Ahmad, 'Evolution of Islamic Banking', p. 354.
4. Gafoor, *Interest Free Commercial Banking*, p. 219.

in there being less demand for the products and services from Islamic windows in conventional banks in comparison to fully-fledged Islamic banks and financial institutions that offer the same products. Any product or service offered by an Islamic bank has to see authorization from the Shariah supervisory authorities that oversee the legitimacy of Shariah compliancy of an investment, product or service.

The growth of Islamic banks around the world and the windows that had been set up to cater for Shariah compliant services are continuing to grow. It is undeniable that the global economic crisis of 2007 further highlighted the benefits of no interest banking that complies with the Shariah and also paved the way for implementation of further Islamic banking services. There are now many fully-fledged Islamic banks around the world spanning the continents of Europe, Asia, the Middle East and the Americas, in addition to financial institutions which offer Shariah compliant services to cater for the growing demand.

2.1 How do Islamic Banks Operate?

The Islamic banking system operates within a framework that adheres to tenet-based principles of Islamic commercial law. The fundamental tenet, which all Islamic banks emphasize, is the prohibition of *ribā* in all equity, asset, liability products and services. The payment or receipt of *ribā* in any form constitutes an invalid transaction, and Islamic banks have to be aware that it must operate without offering any interest-based products, contracts, services or transactions in any form. The absence of *ribā* in Islamic banking poses the question as to how Islamic banks can offer an alternative in comparison to their conventional counterpart, in order to offer a viable alternative for capital and international financial markets and investors. This is where the

Islamic financial principle of profit-and-loss sharing under the *muḍārabah* contract comes into practice, as all Islamic banks have to operate with the implementation of profit-and-loss sharing in replacement of an interest-based system.

All Islamic banks have to adhere to the prohibition of a fixed payment or any acceptance of interest for loans of money in their operations, as a Shariah compliant bank that adheres to the principles of Islamic finance. An Islamic banking institution not only seeks to make money for the banking institute by lending out on capital but also adheres to the ethical principles set out by the Shariah. According to Islam, it is prohibited to lend money with interest and Islam sets out the rules on this in order to prevent *ribā*-based transactions. Islamic banks work in accordance with a profit and risk sharing strategy and use it as a method of trading rather than transferring risk, which is often witnessed within conventional banking institutions. The concept of profit-and-loss sharing utilized through the *muḍārabah* contract is implemented in the smooth running of a fully-fledged Islamic bank. Other key concepts which may be used in the operations of Islamic banks are *wadī'ah*, which is safekeeping; *mushārakah*, which determines joint ventures; *murābaḥah*, the cost plus; and *ijārah*, which means leasing in Arabic.

An Islamic bank works differently in offering a different method of order from conventional banking products and transactions. Islamic banks that are selling a product such as an Islamic mortgage may buy the property from the seller outright and then go on to resell the property to the potential buyer so that it avoids the payment of *ribā* or loans of excess profit. The buyer is then given the option to pay rent to the Islamic bank. This type of transaction ensures that the buyer does not need to pay any excess charges and provides an ethical means of acquiring a property. The Shariah has identified permissible means for acquiring property and Islamic banks cater to provide the opportunity for individuals to obtain a property whilst adhering to their faith.

Islamic banks operate on ethical and socially responsible principles whereby if a buyer cannot afford to pay the monthly rent of the property they are not to be charged additional penalties for late payment, unlike conventional banks which build up interest and increase the customer's debt. However, due to the exposure of liquidity risk, Shariah scholars have allowed charging a penalty, which is not considered as a part of the bank's profit but is a necessary tool, and the money thus generated is distributed to charities. In addition, Islamic banks protect themselves against default, as in the case when a buyer cannot pay an instalment, by asking for strict collateral so that the property, land or products purchased are registered to the name of the buyer from the very beginning of the initial transaction. Islamic banks also have other options to offer its customers, which are similar to real estate leasing. An Islamic bank wishing to offer a loan for a vehicle, for example, may want to use the *ijārah wa iqtinā'* contract which allows the bank to sell the product at a higher price than the current market sells it at until the buyer can afford to pay for it. The ownership of the product will remain with the Islamic bank until the product has been fully paid for.

The aim of Islamic banking is not just to serve as a financial institution for its customers but also to promote the principles governed by Islam, which involves ethical investments and moral purchasing of products. Islamic banks and Shariah compliant financial institutions that offer Islamic banking products and services are expected to establish or refer to a Shariah Supervisory Board (SSB). The role of the SSB to Islamic banks and financial institutions is to advise them on their operations and activities of the bank and ensure Shariah compliancy in all forms of product offerings, investments or transactions.

The SSB of an Islamic bank or financial institution can only advise and issue the legitimacy of a product or service based on the general consensus of the members of the board or referral to expert scholars. All passing of judgement on potential Islamic products and contracts are decided by the board or authority of the bank and have to refer to the ethical principles of Shariah compliant financing based on the tenets of Islam. There are a number of Shariah advisory boards and institutions, which are now rapidly emerging to offer Shariah advisory services to Islamic banks and institutions that offer Islamic financial services.

The Islamic banking system may not be able to guarantee any fixed rate of return on a deposit made, nor can it guarantee the capital gains due to the risks of losses which would inevitably have to be deducted from the capital of the bank. This main difference of operations between Islamic banks and conventional banks results in some countries around the world, which comply with conventional laws, being unable to permit Shariah compliant institutions or banks wishing to implement the profit-and-loss scheme, which ensures the operation of Islamic banking.

Islamic banks operate with a variety of sources of funds to offer their customers. These sources of funds include current accounts, saving accounts, and investment accounts, and limited, unlimited and specified deposit investments from depositors. Islamic banks do not pay interest on any form of deposits but gain their funds through different approaches altogether. The exclusion of *ribā* can be noted through all transactions, sources of funds and product offerings that Islamic banks and financial institutions have to offer in operating a fully-fledged Islamic bank.

Many Islamic banks that have been set up in Islamic financial hubs such as Malaysia and the UAE have prospered in offering innovative Shariah compliant products and services. This has led to the popularity and sustained use of the Islamic bank not only for people who want to utilize Islamic banking in adherence to their faith but also for those who find it an ethically beneficial way of managing finances. Some renowned Islamic banks that have seen success in Shariah compliant banking are the Islamic Development Bank, Dubai Islamic Bank, Bank Islam Malaysia Berhad, Meezan Bank and Al-Rajhi, among others. The global growth of Islamic banks has flourished since their initial emergence in the 1970s, and they can only prosper if Islamic banks operate in a Shariah compliant manner, adhering to the methods of financing laid out by the principles of Islam. Islamic banking continues to provide an ethical alternative to conventional banking, which not only enables Muslims to follow the principles of financing according to their faith but also provides a responsible means of banking for people of all faiths who want to follow an alternative to conventional interest-based financing.

2.2 Islamic and Conventional Banking

Islamic banking is based upon the tenets of Islamic law, which promotes value-based economy, as opposed to the capitalist system, which is a value-free economic model. The main underlying difference between the financial institutions of these two economic models is the absence of *ribā* and the Islamic principles which make Islamic finance a means to better the society at large. The prohibition of *ribā* in Islamic finance plays a crucial role in the operations and ethical morals of an Islamic financial institution, particularly in Islamic banks. Islamic finance does not include or accept the conventional banking method of charging interest for any transaction, whereas conventional banks promote a variety of interest-based products. There may be some Islamic commercial banks that offer products which seem similar to those offered by conventional banks; however, the two entities differ conceptually.

One significant difference is that conventional banks earn profits by charging interest and fees for their products and services, in contrast to Islamic banks which adhere to the principles of the Shariah and earn their money by the scheme of profit-and-loss sharing. Islamic banks also use leasing, charging fees for services rendered, trading and various other Shariah-based contracts of exchange when seeking funds. Another major difference between conventional banking and Islamic banking is the regulation by a Shariah board to determine compliance of transactions, investments, products or services.

It is a prerequisite for any Islamic bank or Islamic financial institution to refer to a Shariah supervisory board or authority in passing judgment on the legitimacy of any product or transaction of the institution. The board normally consists of expert Islamic scholars who are qualified to pass an opinion on whether a product, service or business transaction is Shariah compliant. In an Islamic commercial bank, the board is also involved in supervising bank operations to ensure the bank is operating its services in a wholly Shariah compliant manner.

The prohibition and absence of interest in all Islamic banking institution's contracts, products and services is not the only issue that needs to be overseen. Shariah supervisory boards of Islamic banks also need to ensure that all business contracts, financial instruments and operations of the Islamic institution adhere to the key principles of Islamic finance. These key principles include avoiding speculation or uncertainty, avoiding gambling products and ensuring that all investments are ethical and socially responsible. All investments or loans issued by an Islamic bank have to be used on only permissible products, which comply with the laws of the Shariah, and avoid impermissible industries that go against the core values and tenets of Islam. In contrast, conventional banks can make investments or fund loans on any type of industry or product, even if the industry or service is unethical, immoral or harmful to society. Due to the awareness of socio-economical values and morals that Islamic banking adheres to, it would not be permissible for Islamic banks to follow conventional banks in investing or funding in any industry that they wish just to obtain profits.

The Shariah supervisory board is the backbone of an Islamic banking institution and plays a crucial role in the product offerings and operations of the bank. In comparison, conventional banks do not have the oversight of a supervisory board that determines what investments they can fund and are therefore free to invest in any kind of financial ventures.

There are many other fundamental differences between the two entities of Islamic and conventional banking. The purposes of Islamic and conventional banks differ significantly. The basic purpose for establishing an Islamic bank is to promote and encourage the human-centric development of Muslim communities and is not focused on merely obtaining profits. On the other hand, conventional banks have the primary purpose of making profits that are generally not based on any set of religious principles that govern what is ethical, responsible or moral to society at large. Although there is a major difference in the two underlying values of profit making between Islamic and conventional banking, there is also the fact that commercial Islamic banks do also seek to earn money. Although Islamic banks have a religious obligation to fulfil, it also has to balance this with meeting the objectives of earning money in a Shariah compliant manner.

Islamic banks and financial institutions follow *fiqh al-mu'amālāt* (Islamic commercial law). In addition, Islamic banks also follow the financial laws and regulations of their own respective countries in which they are operating. *Fiqh* essentially means the understanding of Islamic rulings and precepts and in Islamic finance it covers the rulings that govern the financial rights and obligations between individuals. Similarly, conventional banks operate based on their respective country's financial laws and regulations, but they do not have any connection with any specific religious authority to govern permissibility of products or transactions. Hence the main difference comes from adopting these values or not.

The management and relationship between the clients and customers in an Islamic bank also differ from that of conventional banks. For example, conventional banks rely on the system of creditor to debtor when paying in a cheque or a sum of money into the bank. This means that conventional banks have the responsibility to pay back your money either with interest or without it, according to your individual circumstances. When you take up a loan in a conventional bank, the customer becomes indebted to the bank and the bank becomes the creditor, but the conventional bank profits in excess funds due to the issuance of interest on your transaction. This is an unethical and unjust way of obtaining funds that have often left customers heavily in debt, especially if they cannot keep up with their payments.

In addition, any investment made in a conventional bank is based on a guaranteed or fixed income of profit between the bank and the customer. In Islamic banking, the concept of investment follows a different system from that of conventional banking. Although the customer may make an investment, or deposit money in order to earn extra income, the return of a profit may not be guaranteed due to risk sharing and the profit-and-loss sharing mechanism. Depositors may have to bear the losses and the risks are shared equally, in contrast to conventional banks which provide higher return to the depositors with the issuance of guaranteed interest.

Conventional banking institutions often offer an overdraft, where the customer can withdraw excess funds from their account but have to pay back the money with interest, or credit cards in order to satisfy the needs of those who may need an extended amount of money which can be overdrawn, and the bank sets the limit by which a person can overdraw. Islamic banks, however, do not offer this facility since conventional banks primarily rely on interest in order to provide these services and also promote a capitalist system, which could lead to more debt if the amount rises beyond a person's means. The only facility of financing offered by Islamic banks as an alternative is the *murābahah* facility, which means that the Islamic bank will issue the desired commodity a person wants but not the actual money. The basic difference between a conventional overdraft and an Islamic finance alternative lies in the contract being used. *Murābahah* works as a sale contract whereas a conventional overdraft facility is an interest-based lending agreement and transaction.

If a customer has a credit balance they are able to use a debit card in an Islamic bank. Under the *murābahah* facility profits are only due when a commodity is given to the customer[5] and unlike conventional banks default charges are not permissible under the principles of the Shariah. Although there are significant differences that set Islamic banking apart from conventional banking there are also a few similarities, which can be explored. Both Islamic and conventional banks operate within the same society, and both are trying to provide financial assistance, but each are slightly different as the underlying features of financial products offered by Islamic banks are determined by legal injunctions of Islamic law. Another similarity is that deposits can be taken from customers under both conventional and

---

5. M. Hanif, 'Differences and Similarities in Islamic and Conventional Banking', p. 169.

Islamic institutions. Both Islamic banks and conventional banks provide a form of credit-based facility to their customers, however Islamic banks can only issue loans which are free from *ribā*. Both types of bank also provide various means of financing, but work differently in the functioning of offering financing options. It could be noted that there are predominantly more differences than similarities between Islamic banking and finance as the main purpose, values and core operations differ considerably.

It may be important to consider the fact that Islamic banking is always asset-based, which means that all of its transactions require the support of assets. There are also other elements to Islamic banks, such as the services for giving zakat, which constitutes charity based on the Islamic faith that conventional banks do not promote, nor do conventional banks offer ethically-based products based on any form of religious principles or moral socio-economic values. Islamic banks, however, do cater for ethically-based products and services with the promotion of preventing debt through the absence of interest.

Islamic banking is not confined to catering for Muslims alone, as non-Muslims are also encouraged to benefit from socially responsible banking that provides morally attractive financial options for its customers. Conventional banks do not cater for those Muslims who want to adhere to the principles of the Islamic faith in their financial transactions because conventional banking relies heavily upon a variety of interest-based products. Although there are products offered by conventional banks which may be interest free, there are no other clear alternatives for Muslim customers in determining the true legitimacy of whether the product is Shariah compliant or not. Islamic banking, however, does cater to adhere to the principles of the Shariah, as this is what governs the whole Islamic banking system in its functioning and operation as a Shariah compliant financial institution.

Following the global economic crisis of 2007, Islamic banking was brought into the spotlight and highlighted as a viable alternative to conventional banking. The benefits of no interest banking became more appealing to those who had fallen heavily into debt through the products and services of conventional banks. The global appetite for Islamic banking has grown through the years and there is an increasing need for financial services to cater for the demand for Shariah compliant banking products. This is why there have been many conventional banks that have tried to implement Shariah compliant windows, which offer services in this niche sector.

However, there may be challenges in implementing a financial system of Islamic banking products within a conventional bank, as the core values are different. With a rise in the development of innovative Shariah compliant banking products and services there is more scope for Islamic banking to flourish in the years to come. The increasing number of people who have used interest-based products and fallen heavily into debt has shaped an economic downfall in financial stability. Islamic banking based on no-interest policies could have the potential to restore financial stability and offer a viable alternative to managing finances responsibly. Islamic banking could also exponentially cater in offering services that can combat poverty. Many Islamic microfinancing organizations have been developed to tackle poverty and create a better life for the community at large. In addition, Islamic banking can aim to alleviate the misuse of financing and promote more socially responsible forms of banking.

CHAPTER 3

Financial Instruments

Instruments of Islamic finance are used to cater for the functioning of services that an Islamic bank has to offer. In many Muslim countries around the world government securities of financial instruments are traded at a smaller level and prohibited interest-based products are often marketed. Islamic financial instruments are predominantly equity-based and follow the system of profit-and-loss sharing and the equal sharing of risks between two parties. Equity markets are considered to be as beneficial investments by Islamic financial institutions in comparison to conventional government securities. The challenge of marketable Islamic financial instruments is often a concern when weighing up its profitability. It is a requirement of all Islamic banks and financial institutions to operate without any *ribā*-based deposits or government securities, which include interest. Islamic financial instruments are predominantly used to trade.

The economist Rodney Wilson outlined two possible Islamic financial instruments which could ensure more profitability for Islamic banks: The creation of Islamic certificates of deposit, which could be traded amongst the Islamic banks,[1] and the issuance of Shariah compliant debt instruments by the governments of Muslim states, which could spur profitability in trading. In order for Islamic financial instruments to be traded successfully there needs to be an existence of sufficient buyers and sellers. The requirement to adhere to the principles of Shariah compliant financing has shaped the Islamic financial instruments of today and are used to facilitate proper conduct and usage of an Islamic financial institution. Islamic banking institutions are required to adhere to running their banks without the sole purpose of profit-making, without charging interest and with the promotion of delivering investments which have benefits for the community and society at large. The concept of risk sharing has formed the basis for Islamic financial instruments such as *muḍārabah*, which is one of the main instruments that will be discussed in more detail in the subsequent sections.

Islamic banking instruments enable customers to benefit from a growing range of Shariah compliant products and services, which are ethically-based along socially responsible principles. In addition, many instruments encourage long term partnerships between two parties – the client and the bank – due to the nature of the contracts. Islamic financial instruments are highly ethical since Islamic banks are not solely focused on profit-making, unlike their conventional counterparts whose primary purpose is to make money through any form of investment, industry or product.

Some of the challenges posed in implementing Islamic financial instruments constitute what is deemed legitimately

---

1. R. Wilson, *Development of Financial Instruments in an Islamic Frame-work*, pp. 2

to Have read.
a read

Shariah compliant and what is not. Therefore, some Islamic financial institutions may agree that specific instruments are permissible while others may argue that they are not. This poses a challenge of standardization, which needs to be overcome, in order for more new and innovative products to be developed and for the Islamic financial industry to see a sustained growth in the development of financial instruments.

3.1 Key Financial Instruments in Islamic Finance and Banking

There are a number of key financial instruments which are used in Islamic finance and banking, and in this section of the book we will discuss those that are most commonly used. It is important to note that innovative Islamic financial instruments are continually being formed in order to cater for the progress of Islamic banking and to spur the growth of the Islamic finance industry. The basic functions in which an Islamic bank or financial institution operates is through the principles of the Shariah and are built upon schemes such as profit-and-loss sharing, as we have discussed earlier. However, there are other Islamic financial instruments which cater to fulfil these functions in order to aid in delivering the services of an Islamic finance institution in a Shariah compliant manner, as discussed in the next sections. Please note that the inclusion of key financial instruments such as *bay' al-'inah*, *tawarruq* and *bay' bithaman 'ājil* that are used in some Islamic banks are not considered permissible by some scholars but are included so that the reader can identify and be aware of these innovative modes of financial instrument.

3.2 *Muḍārabah*

Muḍārabah is a special partnership used by the Islamic banking sector for investment in a commercial enterprise. A *muḍārabah* contract is based on an investment partnership between two parties; the *rab al-māl*, who provides the capital, and the *muḍārib*, who uses it for the business. In a *muḍārabah* contract, one of the partners – who is in many cases an entrepreneur – has expertise to offer in implementing the venture capital into the economic activity which is to be funded. Both parties involved in the *muḍārabah* contract have to agree in advance to comply with the Shariah compliant principles of profit-and-loss sharing. In accordance with the *muḍārabah* contract, the Islamic economics system considers that there should be some basic processes of production, such as implementing entrepreneurship and capital and doing the work effectively, in order to constitute economic activity. The *rab al-māl* ensures to fund the capital, and the *muḍārib* provides the skill or expertise in the form of entrepreneurship and labour.

All *muḍārabah* contracts are bound by a specific length of time and do not have an unlimited time span. According to the principles of Shariah compliant financing, *muḍārabah* is a permissible Islamic financial contract and has been approved by the consensus of scholars. The profits obtained through the Islamic financial instrument of *muḍārabah* are shared with the manager, the *muḍārib*, and the capital provider, *rab al-māl*, but only the capital provider – who adheres to the profit-and-loss sharing mechanism – endures the losses.

Muḍārabah contracts can also operate as a source of funding for an Islamic bank or financial institution. When a customer decides to make a deposit to the Islamic banking institution and expect a return, they are considered to be the *rab al-māl*, which means in Arabic the 'investors'. The Islamic bank invests the customer's money according to the principles of Sharia compliant financing in a *muḍārabah* contract.

There are two types of *muḍārabah* contracts that a person can choose to invest in: restricted *muḍārabah* and unrestricted *muḍārabah* – also known as *muḍārabah al-muqayadah* and *muḍārabah al-mutlaqh*.[2] In the restricted *muḍārabah*, the investor can choose which investment project they would like to utilize the funds in and the partner cannot use the funds for any other project. In the unrestricted *muḍārabah* contract, the investor gives flexibility to the working partner and makes any type of Shariah compliant investment project or business permissible. This allows the working partner to utilize the funds given to them in any business or project and they have the freedom to choose where they spend the funds. With *muḍārabah* contracts, the *rab al-māl* and the *muḍārib* share all the profits and losses. The *muḍārabah* contract adheres to the profit-and-loss sharing scheme quite strictly.

Another *muḍārabah* contract that is also offered by Islamic banks is the intermediary *muḍārabah*, which is also known as a two-tier contract. The intermediary *muḍārabah* contract operates as the Islamic bank taking on the role of intermediary between the depositor and the customer. Intermediary *muḍārabah* contracts are often used in cases when an Islamic bank or institution does not have the capacity to take on the role of the *rab al-māl*. In most cases, when this type of *muḍārabah* contract exists the Islamic banking institution does not have sufficient means of liquidity to enter into a *muḍārabah* contract with an entrepreneur or funding manager. In addition, the Islamic bank may not have the expertise to function as a fund manager to cover the overall investment project or business.

---

2.   F. Jamaldeen, 'The Mudaraba Contract in Islamic Finance', p. 87.

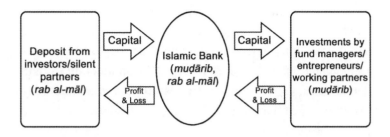

Figure 3.1: The two-tier *Muḍārabah* Contract for an Islamic Bank

An intermediary *muḍārabah* contract, as shown in Figure 3.1, enables the Islamic bank to create a direct link between an investor and the entrepreneur or funding manager in order for Shariah compliant economic activity to function. Although the option of an intermediary *muḍārabah* is available, the straightforward *muḍārabah* contract involving only the bank as a fund manager and the customer is more commonly used.

Main supply chain
→ financing tool.

3.3 *Murābaḥah*

Murābaḥah works as a cost-plus type of transaction or agreement whereby a commodity is sold for a cost plus profit by the bank. The buyer and seller agree on a predetermined cost and profit involved, and that is outlined in the contract. Many Islamic banks offer *murābaḥah* as a trade-financing Islamic financial instrument.

The *murābaḥah* contract acts as a financial instrument for an Islamic bank that can purchase a commodity at full value and then offer it to customers who may not be able to finance the whole commodity themselves. The Islamic bank or institution can sell the commodity to the customer on a cost-plus profit basis, whereby the profit is predetermined and agreed upon by both parties, which are the bank and the customer. Under a *murābaḥah* contract a customer can pay in instalments, if they cannot financially pay the amount up-front, or they can make a full payment when they have received the commodity from the Islamic bank. One distinguishing feature of *murābaḥah* is that the seller is transparent in informing the purchaser how much cost he has incurred and how much profit he is going to charge.

The absence of uncertainty complies with the principles of Shariah financing, as everything is agreed upon when the customer signs the initial contract, which can prevent against any debt in the transaction. An example of a *murābaḥah* contract is if a builder wants to buy £50,000 worth of bricks but does not have enough money to purchase them. The builder may turn to an Islamic bank and sign a *murābaḥah* contract. The builder can agree to buy the bricks at £50,000 and add an additional profit of £10,000 for the bank – so the overall price they would pay is £60,000. The price of the product and the profit that the bank will receive is stated at the onset and agreed upon by the two parties, and this is how a *murābaḥah* contract works. The builder in this example is liable to pay the amount stated in the contract to the bank when the bank hands over the commodity.

Murābaḥah is a popular financial instrument that has numerous advantages. For example, the risk-bearing period for the financier is significantly shorter than other financing instruments. In addition, the financier also identifies its profit as soon as the *murābaḥah* transaction is complete, which enables greater transparency throughout the contract. However, the implementation of a *murābaḥah* contract does expose an Islamic financial institution to potential credit risks arising from a customer who is unable to settle the outstanding debt obligation. Many Islamic financial institutions have therefore made it pertinent to establish a comprehensive risk management framework to ensure support mechanisms are available if an issue of default was to arise.

The *murābaḥah* contract can be used by banks as an Islamic financial instrument; however, there are some regulations which need to be applied in order to maintain Shariah compliancy of the transaction. For example, if the customer defaults in payment the Islamic bank is not allowed to charge them any *ribā*, as it is strictly prohibited to charge *ribā* and gain excess profits under Shariah law. The bank may be allowed to issue penalties but it will not be allowed to use any of this money as profit and may ask the customer to give the amount as charity. Under Shariah compliant banking, the *murābaḥah* contract should only be used on purchases of a working capital nature.

There are two main types of *murābaḥah* contracts that an Islamic bank may offer to its customers. A customer may want to order a specific number of goods at a fixed price and request the bank to purchase the goods on their behalf and buy them back from the bank at the price agreed. This type of *murābaḥah* transaction is a *murābaḥah* to a purchase order. Another type of contract, which is often regarded as impermissible, is the commodity *murābaḥah*, which relies upon being used as a financial instrument in aiding Islamic interbank transactions to fund the bank's liquidity under a short term period. The commodity *murābaḥah* was established as an alternative to conventional funding between banks. However, although some Islamic financial institutions have offered commodity *murābaḥah*, it has faced extreme criticism as it is argued that this is a pre-arranged transaction that has no economic value and is meant to create debt without the ability to separate the sale and the buy-back contract.

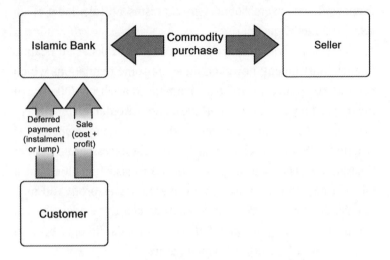

Figure 3.2: The *Murābaḥah* Contract in an Islamic Bank

Although there remains some misunderstandings regarding the Islamic financial instrument of *murābaḥah*, the instrument itself is widely used and does aim to fulfil Shariah compliancy, distinguishing itself from conventional financing if all Islamic principles are met. For example, an Islamic bank purchases an asset on the customer's behalf, so there are no loans involved in contrast to conventional banks who loan the money to the customer. In addition, the cost and profit of the purchase is already predetermined and agreed by both the customer and the bank, so there is no uncertainty in the financial transaction. If the customer fails to meet the payment instalments required by the Islamic bank they are not liable to pay excess amounts of money to the bank, unlike conventional banks which often operate on charging additional interest and gain from the profits of interest. The system of economic activity that the Shariah underscores ensures that all assets are real when traded, unlike conventional banks that issue loans without any regard for the activity used. *Murābaḥah* is being offered by increasing numbers of Islamic banks around the world as a tangible Islamic financial instrument.

3.4 *Ijārah*

Ijārah is an Arabic term which literally means 'leasing' or to rent or hire. The Islamic financial instrument of *ijārah* is used predominantly in Islamic banks and financial institutions to provide a service or goods over a temporary time period for a payment. The *ijārah* contract is reliant upon providing products, goods or services on a lease or hire basis. The concept of *ijārah* enables an individual to rent out a product or service over a specified period of time and allows the owner of the product to have full ownership over the assets.

The *ijārah* financial contract operates by leasing a product, goods or property to an individual for a specified period of time in exchange for a payment. The person who is leasing the product, property or goods must follow the principles of the Shariah to fulfil the *ijārah* contract, and it is therefore compulsory for them to own the assets for the full duration of the period of the lease. As the charging of interest is prohibited under Shariah law, the person who is renting a product may not be charged any additional payments in the case of default but instead assets may be taken to avoid negligence. The *ijārah* contract has to specifically outline the use of the asset that is going to be leased, as its primary use is important in complying with the principles of the Shariah.

Conventional leasing works in a similar way, by enabling the rental of a property or product for a fee. However, conventional banks charge interest and the bank is allowed to profit from any interest charged on the transaction – in contrast to Islamic banks, which do not charge excess amounts under the *ijārah* ruling. There are different types of *ijārah* that can be utilized according to the principles of the Shariah, such as *ijārah wa iqtinā'*, which means lease ending with ownership, or ownership with the lease. In this type of *ijārah* contract the person who is hiring the product will become the owner of the asset once at the end of the lease period. *Ijārah wa iqtinā'* is most likely to be offered to home owners wishing to finance their house in a Shariah compliant manner. The Islamic bank will not guarantee buying or selling of the asset but will be able to schedule the duration of time that a person can lease the asset until he or she fully acquires it. In this case, the person leasing the product is also allowed to make a verbal intention to the Islamic bank to purchase the asset at its current market value or at a price which is agreed upon by both the bank and the individual who wants to lease.

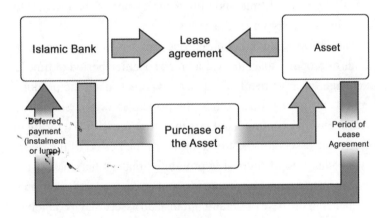

Figure 3.3: An *Ijārah* Operating Lease Contract

Another form of *ijārah* contract is an operating *ijārah*, which means that there is no guarantee to purchase the asset at the end of the duration of the contract. Hence this is more of a hiring scheme between the bank and the customer and may be used for the hiring of goods over a period of time that will not be needed once the contract ends, and therefore there is no necessity to purchase. An operating *ijārah* contract does not end with the transfer of ownership of leased assets to the lessee, unlike a financial *ijārah* whereby the ownership is given to the lessee at the end of the contract.

The *ijārah* contract complies with the Shariah if it is used accordingly, and *ijārah* is one of the most popular types of financing instruments that Islamic financial institutions use. *Ijārah* as a financial instrument has developed and grown in popularity as a successful instrument by both global Islamic banks and financial institutions. There are many forms and contracts of *ijārah* which can be utilized for different purposes and this is one of the reasons it makes the instrument such a successful product in Islamic banks and institutions. The majority of Muslim scholars are of the opinion that the *ijārah* contract is fully compliant with the principles of Shariah compliant financing and adheres to the tenets of Islam. This is because that there are many verses from the holy Qur'an and the Prophetic Sunnah that give evidence of permissibility to use *ijārah* in Islamic finance and banking.

3.5 *Istisnā'*

Istisnā' is a form of forward sales contract over a long-term duration between a buyer and seller. It is primarily used for the purpose of construction-based projects, which are contracted to be delivered at a future date in exchange for a predetermined price. Both the Islamic bank and the customer has to agree on the future date and price and this has to be outlined in the *istisnā'* contract at the onset, as shown in Figure 3.4. The project specifications also have to be written into the *istisnā'* contract so that if the customer feels that the project does not meet the specifications they are eligible to leave the contract.

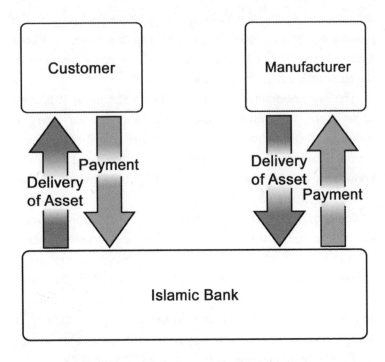

Figure 3.4: The Parallel *Istiṣnā'* in Islamic Banks

Istiṣnā' is a flexible financial instrument as it allows the manufacturer of a product or service to complete a construction project at a future agreed time with flexible payment options between both parties. Under the *istiṣnā'* contract the price is agreed before the asset that is outlined in the agreement is actually constructed. Sellers have the flexibility to create the asset or construction themselves or to sub-contract to another party to build it according to the project specifications outlined in the contract. The buyers have the flexibility of paying the seller either in instalments during the construction work or in advance before the project has been completed, according to their individual preferences.

In Arabic, *istiṣnā'* means to 'ask someone to manufacture' and is a common Islamic financial instrument used by construction or infrastructure industries through Islamic banks. Both parties are eligible to state the best method of payment, according to their individual requirements, and there is no pressure on the buyer to pay the seller in advance. The *istiṣnā'* financial instrument is widely used in trade and project finance industries including those that create projects for building housing schemes or residential complexes.

As uncertainty of any transaction or product is prohibited under the principles of Shariah compliant financing, the *istiṣnā'* contract has to be fully transparent and detailed in outlining what the end product will be like. This ensures that the customer is satisfied with every detail of the product to be made and can enter into the contract with full knowledge of what is planned for the end product. The *istiṣnā'* contract operates by the use of an Islamic bank where the customer presents the specification for the asset and signs an *istiṣnā'* agreement contract. The Islamic bank then manufactures the asset for the customer through a specified manufacturer who can carry out the work according to the specifications outlined in the contract.

3.6 *Salam*

The Islamic financial instrument of *salam* operates as a forward sales contract or financing transaction, where the financial institution pays in advance for buying specified assets. *Salam* is similar to *istiṣnā'*, in fact they both operate under the forward sales contract scheme, whereby the seller will supply the asset on a predetermined date. According to the principles of Shariah compliant financing, both parties need to agree on the future date for the delivery of the goods and outline the specifications for the exact quantity or quality of the product they wish acquire.

Some Muslim jurists dispute over the permissibility of the *salam* contract as it may be considered to constitute a type of debt, because the Islamic bank has already made the payment and the seller is liable to deliver the goods that was agreed upon. There is generally a consensus among Muslim jurists that the issuance of a *salam* contract does not comply with the principles of the Shariah. This is due to the fact that the Shariah does not allow the sale of a commodity which is not already owned by the seller, because the objectives of the contract is that the assets are a recompense for the initial price that was paid in advance.

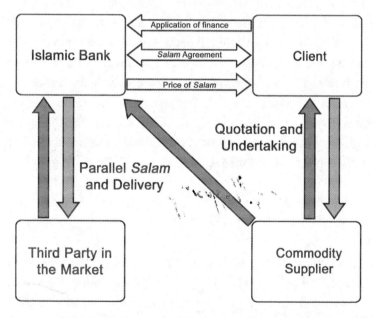

Figure 3.5: The *Salam* Process in an Islamic Bank

The *salam* transaction is only considered legitimate if the buyer has paid the full amount of the price of the asset to the seller at the time of the initial sale. The utilization of the *salam* contract works conceptually as a mechanism that ensures that the seller achieves the liquidity they expected from entering into the transaction. Muslim scholars are unanimous that full payment of the purchase price is essential for *salam* to exist. However, *salam* cannot take place in actual currency because the asset has not yet been created and does not exist. Since *salam* primarily involves the delivery of a product or asset, which is non-existent, there are a few rules and regulations that the Shariah outlines to ensure that both parties are protected. Both parties have to agree on predetermined specifications for the commodity so that there is no uncertainty, which is also prohibited under the laws of the Shariah. There should also be no space for ambiguity of the product specification, and the requirements of the commodity should be outlined in the *salam* contract before both parties sign it.

The commodity offered through the *salam* contract should be available in the market at the time of delivery to the buyer. The specification of the assets in the *salam* contract have to be specified and detail should be taken in covering all aspects of the product specification in order to prevent disputes and to avoid a variation in the price paid.

I'e still r. confusing

3.7 *Mushārakah*

The literal definition of *mushārakah* in Arabic means 'sharing'. However, *mushārakah* as a Islamic financial instrument refers to a 'joint partnership where two or more persons combine either their capital or labour, forming a business in which all partners share the profit according to a specific ratio, while the loss is shared according to the ratio of the contribution'.[3]

---

3.   M. I. Usmani, 'Musharakah', p. 87.

The Islamic financial instrument of *mushārakah* operates predominantly through Islamic banks and is a joint partnership between two parties or more that contribute an amount of capital into an investment and share the net profit-and-loss on a *pro rata* basis. The *mushārakah* contract is often used for the purpose of investment projects since it can include more than one party who will contribute capital to the overall project. Another example where *mushārakah* may be used is in the real estate or property sector, where the bank will operate on a rental basis and share the profit as agreed in the contract.

All of the contributors of capital under a *mushārakah* contract are expected to participate in the overall management of the investment. Any profits gained through the *mushārakah* financial contract have to be distributed among each participant in ratios that were specified at the time of signing the contract. If there are any losses incurred, each partner has to bear the loss in the proportion of their own respective contribution, which they made initially to the capital for the project or investment. The concept of *mushārakah* is unique in comparison to conventional fixed income investing such as with a fixed loan.

Many Islamic banks offer their customers another type of *mushārakah* financial instrument, which uses an equity participation system. In this type of transaction the joint venture partnership is based around the economic activity that occurs between the Islamic bank and the customer. In this partnership all the parties have to contribute a portion towards capital, entrepreneurship and labour, which constitutes the Islamic view of economic production (see Figure 3.6). In a *mushārakah* contract all the participants involved are expected to contribute to the investment and are therefore active working partners, unlike in the *muḍārabah* contract where the bank is the silent partner and the other party is the working partner, which provides the economic activity.

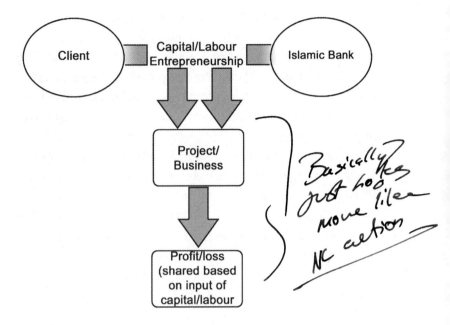

Figure 3.6: The *Mushārakah* in Islamic Banking

A *mushārakah* financial instrument may be used if a company wants to establish a joint venture project with an Islamic bank. They can bring a certain amount of capital to the bank and the Islamic bank will contribute another portion of the capital needed to fund the project. For example, the company could make a £200,000 contribution and the Islamic bank contribute £250,000 to the contract. The company will provide the expertise to oversee the project and get it started, but the Islamic bank's role will be to contribute the remaining capital and be involved in managing some aspects of the project if they wish to do so. Under the *mushārakah* contract the two parties share the profits and bear any losses incurred based upon the capital that they each respectively contributed at the start of the contract. If the joint venture project is successful, and the end product sells at a higher price, then the company will gain and the bank will also gain in profits based on their initial contribution. The same system works for any incurred losses by the Islamic bank and the company.

Islamic banks may also use the *mushārakah* contract in order to facilitate trade financing and provide working capital to support larger based projects or investments. An example of this is when an Islamic bank issues a letter of credit to a customer who deals in trade abroad. In this case the partnership will be a limited partnership that gives the customer the support they need. In this form of *mushārakah* the customer may present with a lack of sufficient funds to obtain what they need and the customer will supply part of the capital whilst the bank supplies the rest of the capital needed. The Islamic bank then can issue the letter of credit and the desired product will be delivered to the customer.

Islamic banks may categorize *mushārakah* products under two main types based upon the duration of time or the period that the partners will stay in the joint venture. These are known as consecutive *mushārakah* and diminishing *mushārakah*. Consecutive *mushārakah* is where both partners keep their respective shares in the partnership until the joint venture project or business is completed. The partners are, however, allowed to take out their share or transfer it providing that this is already declared in the initial contract. Diminishing *mushārakah* is where one partner is eligible to purchase another partners' share of equity through a gradual process until the complete equity amount is transferred. This is also known as a 'declining balance partnership' due to the fact that one partners' equity balance declines through a gradual process.

3.8 *Bay' al-'inah*

Bay' al-'inah is a financial instrument that is used by some Islamic banks and financial institutions, although this instrument has been disputed as being impermissible and not adhering to the Shariah principles of Islamic commercial law. *Bay' al-'inah* provides a facility of finance through a buying and selling transaction between a financier and a customer. The Islamic bank, in this example, buys an asset from the customer and the Islamic bank, constituting any disbursement, pays the price of the asset. The asset is then sold on to the customer through a deferred payment system and the customer is liable to pay the price back in instalments, similar to paying off a loan.

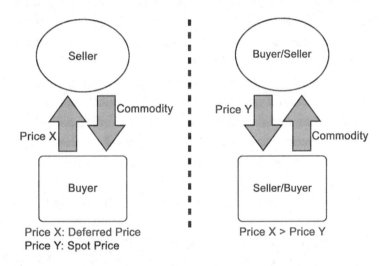

Price X: Deferred Price
Price Y: Spot Price

Price X > Price Y

Figure 3.7: *Bay' al-'Inah* **Sale Transaction in Islamic Banking**

To be considered wholly Shariah compliant under Islamic jurisprudence, the *bay' al-'inah* contract presents a problem, though Malaysia has many Islamic banks that practice *bay' al-'inah* and offer it as an option of financing. Islamic financial institutions who support this mode of financing, which is shown in Figure 3.7, have argued that it is a legitimate instrument because it is a sale transaction. However, Ḥanafī and Ḥanbalī schools view that *bay' al-'inah* is not permissible because the intention will invalidate the contract. They argue that the motive of the parties determines the illegality of the contract.

Bay' al-'inah works as a financial instrument by the process of selling a product and then purchasing it again at a reasonable price. The concept of a *bay' al-'inah* transaction is similar to the *murābaḥah* transaction. In this case, though, the customer has to ensure that they purchase the commodity and then sell it back to the financier or Islamic banking institution for cash, which is almost like the conventional sale and buy-back contracts found in conventional banks, which is why the transaction is disputed. The customer in the *bay' al-'inah* contract will receive the desired amount of cash they need from the sale and then use the deferred payment method to settle the transaction.

Bay' al-'inah involves a process of facilitation, as first the commodity that is owned by the financier is sold to the customer through a deferred payment scheme at a price agreeable to both parties. Secondly, the customer has to pay for the commodity based upon the agreed price, in addition to paying the deferred payment according to the terms outlined in the contract. After the customer has received the commodity, he or she then sells it to the financier immediately but at a discounted price. The financier, i.e. the Islamic bank, has to pay an on-the-spot price and the customer will then acquire the funds. The main purpose behind the *bay' al-'inah* instrument is to establish an amount or price difference between the sales of a commodity to another party, who should always be the same bank or client, by alternating their roles. The difference between the first initial sale that takes place and the second sale constitutes a *bay' al-'inah* transaction, which relies upon a delayed payment back to the bank. In a *bay' al-'inah* contract there is no form of trade and exchange and scholars dispute the authenticity of the concept of *bay' al-'inah*, as the way that the contract is conducted plays a crucial role in determining whether it is Shariah compliant.

3.9 *Bay' bithaman 'ājil*

The *bay' bithaman 'ājil* instrument refers to a credit sale of goods on a deferred payment scheme for a price and an additional profit margin that is agreed upon by the two parties involved in the contract. *Bay' bithaman 'ājil* is primarily used under an Islamic financing facility, such as an Islamic bank. It is often argued that this type of financial instrument is created to be different from conventional interest-based payments, since according to the *bay' bithaman 'ājil* contract, the customer has to pay back the sale price. However, there is a perception amongst scholars that *bay' bithaman 'ājil* goes against the tenets of Islam and Shariah compliant financing, as according to Islamic scholars the contract does charge interest, though it is only termed as a 'sale'. The fact that the bank makes excess profit through the *bay' bithaman 'ājil* and benefits from extra income which is higher than the original price taken from the customer, goes against the principles of Islamic commercial law.

Bay' bithaman 'ājil operates as a repurchasing agreement and is a concept used in Islamic banking that works on a hire purchase finance or purchasing insurance basis. Under *bay' bithaman 'ājil*, the Islamic bank provides the funding to a customer for a service or product in order to purchase the assets from the customer with a cash sum, and then the bank will sell the asset back to the customer based on the purchase price and with excess profit, which does not really comply with the principles of the Shariah according to Islamic jurisprudence. The model of *bay' bithaman 'ājil* as practiced for a home purchase plan is shown in Figure 3.8.

Under a *bay' bithaman 'ājil* contract, customers are entitled to pay the cash amount back to the bank through a deferred payment, which can be paid through a process of instalments. The amount of payment that the customer is liable to pay is based upon the total purchasing costs involved, the payment that is outlined in the initial agreement between the bank and the customer, and the risks involved in the payment.

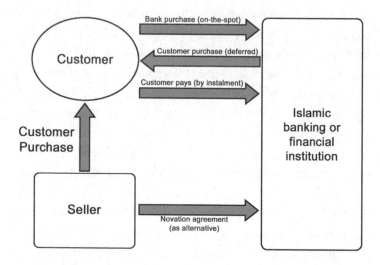

Figure 3.8: *Bay' bithaman 'ājil* **in a Home Purchasing Plan**

The *bay' bithaman 'ājil* is considered by Islamic banks to be an alternative to the conventional banking system of lending; though this is often disputed amongst Islamic economic jurists. *Bay' bithaman 'ājil* was first introduced in Malaysia in 1983 by Bank Islam Malaysia. However, this form of Islamic financial instrument has not been widely accepted and instead other Islamic banks around the world prefer to use the instrument of *murābaḥah* or cost-plus contracts instead.

3.10 *Bay' Muajjal*

The Islamic financial instrument of *bay' muajjal* is a deferred credit sale, the same as *bay' bithaman 'ājil*. This instrument is used predominantly by Islamic banks and utilizes the *murābaḥah* Islamic financial contract. *Bay' muajjal* operates as a contract whereby the Islamic bank gains a profit margin on the purchase price and enables the buyer to make the payment for a commodity at a future date either in full or in instalments. The payment involved in this type of contract has to be specified in the initial contract and the cost of the commodity and marginal profit should be mutually agreed and consented by both parties when signing the contract. The fixed price for the commodity can either be the same as the spot price or it can be increased or decreased according to what is agreed between the two parties.

It is argued among scholars whether *bay' muajjal* genuinely adheres to the principles outlined in the Shariah, because *ribā* is completely prohibited and since a delay in payment that increases the price is permissible under this contract the adherence to Shariah principles comes into question. In order for *bay' muajjal* to work effectively, the contract between the Islamic bank and the customer has to ensure that the bank sells the commodity in accordance to the specified requirements of the customer at the agreed price, which is payable by the customer at a named future date. The purchasing of goods by the Islamic bank should ensure that it is made on behalf of the bank, and in the case where payment of the price of goods is turned into a payment for the customer the excess amount of profit will be considered to constitute *ribā*.

3.11 *Tawarruq*

Tawarruq literally means to convert an asset into money, and operates when a buyer makes a purchase on a commodity from a seller based on a deferred payment method. The buyer then goes on to sell the same commodity to another party using the spot payment method, which means that the payment has to be made there and then. *Tawarruq* is used to enable the buyer to generate the funds they need in order to make the initial purchase of the commodity they wish to buy. A *murābaḥah* contract is used in the latter part of the transaction, when the buyer receives the cash or funds from the bank. The buyer will then pay the seller either in instalments or through a lump sum payment, which can be arranged through a *murābaḥah* or cost-plus transaction agreement.

The process of *tawarruq* is often referred to as making a reverse *murābaḥah*, since the buyer has to make a contract for a *murābaḥah* transaction and then buyer must make the same reversed transaction. In order for *tawarruq* to operate both transactions that are involved under the *murābaḥah* contract must be wholly Shariah compliant. The operationalization of *tawarruq* in Islamic banks is shown in Figure 3.9.

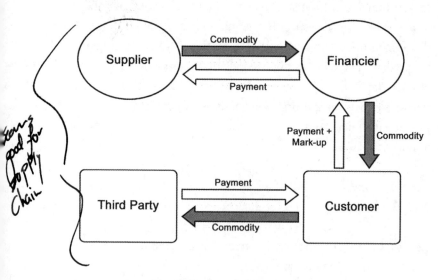

Figure 3.9: *Tawarruq* **in Islamic Banking**

Tawarruq is considered a controversial instrument because of a difference of opinion among scholars regarding the fact that the commodity purchased will not be for the use of the buyer and there is an absence of any real working capital or economic activity. In order for *tawarruq* to be fully Shariah compliant it would need to adhere to the principles of economic activity; if it does not, scholars argue that without any real working economic activity interest will be incurred and that is strictly prohibited under the principles of the Shariah.

Islamic jurists and scholars who accept *tawarruq* have argued that it may be permissible under valid *murābahah* contracts. Despite a difference of opinion on the authenticity of this Islamic financial instrument, there are many Islamic banks that include *tawarruq*-based products in their lists of Islamic financial contracts available to their customers.

Tawarruq was established in order to provide a product that enables customers to obtain cash for a commodity on a deferred payment basis, and the customer gets to turn a commodity into cash using the Islamic bank as an intermediary. The bank used makes a profit from the sale of the commodity and can also act as an agent for selling off the commodity for the customer. An example of how *tawarruq* works is that a bank can purchase the commodity from a trader in the market on a cash basis. The bank or financier then sells the commodity to the customer at cost price plus profit margin, which is to be paid either as a lump sum or in instalments by the customer. If the customer wishes they may ask the bank to act as the agent in selling the commodity to another trader, again within the commodity market on a cash basis.

3.12 *Qarḍ al-Ḥasan*

The *qarḍ al-ḥasan* Islamic financial instrument literally means a 'benevolent loan' in Arabic. This type of loan is given on the principle of good will in order to benefit a person in helping them to finance a socially responsible event or service, which they may be in need of. The *qarḍ al-ḥasan* contract operates on a system where the Islamic bank provides a loan to the customer and the customer is only required to repay the exact amount borrowed. The Islamic bank does not profit from this type of loan and Shariah scholars say that this is the only type of loan that does not go against the principle of the prohibition of *ribā*; it does not truly profit the creditor as the funds are being used to help a person in need.

Qarḍ al-ḥasan loans offered by Islamic banks have been used to provide profit-free financing for marriages, medical treatment or educational expenses amongst many other socially responsible and beneficial industries that benefit the community or society at large. This is why the term for this type of financial instrument is referred to as a loan given by the bank on a good will basis only, and it has to be used on legitimate services or products in accordance with Islamic jurisprudence. The purpose of *qarḍ al-ḥasan* is to aid people in need and works with the aim of protecting them from exploitation by other money lenders.

3.13 *Wadī'ah*

Wadī'ah in Arabic literally means 'safekeeping' and is an Islamic financial instrument used by Islamic banks whereby the bank is considered to be the keeper and trustee of a specific amount of funds. An example of *wadī'ah* is when a person deposits an amount of funds into an Islamic bank and the bank acts as a trustee of the deposit to ensure that the person will be refunded the entire amount or any part of the amount that the depositor desires.

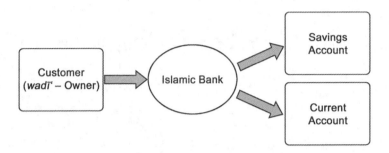

Figure 3.10: *Wadī'ah* in Islamic Banking

Many Islamic banks offer *wadī'ah* accounts to their customers and provide them with a mode of deposit governed by the principles of *wadī'ah*, which are based upon the Islamic Shariah. The Islamic bank is liable to pay the refund, which should be guaranteed by the bank to the depositor, and the depositor may also receive a profit reward for making a deposit in the bank, according to the bank's management. Islamic banks normally offer *wadī'ah* through a deposit account and a receipt may be issued to the customer by the Islamic bank for each deposit made under the *wadī'ah* account system.

3.14 *Wakālah*

Wakālah is literally an agency contract and exists when a person appoints someone else to represent them either in managing their finances or providing legal action. The representative is required to undertake transactions on the person's behalf, which is similar to the conventional method of power of attorney. *Wakālah* operates as a contract from Islamic banks whereby the bank will issue a contract between a principle and third party for a fixed agreed amount.

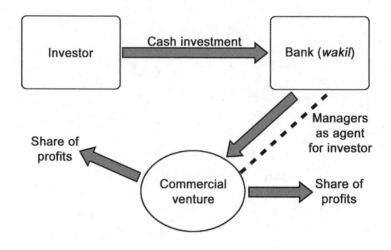

Figure 3.11: *Wakālah* **in Islamic Banking**

In Islamic banking *wakālah* is concerned with the provision of a service that could include a sale and purchase, rental and hire, borrowing and lending and guarantees. Islamic banks can use the concept of *wakālah* in many Islamic products such as *mushārakah*, *ijārah*, *muḍārabah*, *murābaḥah*, *salam* and *istiṣnā'*. It can also be utilized when the bank wants to collect trading bills or become involved in fund management. Islamic banks normally charge a fee for the services of an agent, which is rendered by the bank on behalf of a client. In any *wakālah* contract all terms can be specified in order to avoid any future disputes between the client and the representative.

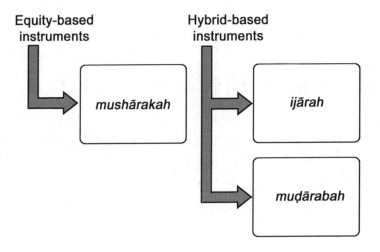

Figure 3.12: A Summary of Key Islamic Financial Instruments

CHAPTER 4

Islamic Financial Contracts

4.1 An Ethical Choice

Islamic financial contracts play a crucial role in the facilitation of products, profit and services in an Islamic bank or financial institution. All Islamic financial contracts have to be based upon the principles of the Shariah and adhere to the tenets that Islam has outlined in both the Qur'an and Sunnah. As Islamic banks facilitate many Shariah compliant financial contracts, these provide an alternative way of financing to conventional financial contracts.

There have been various practices and interpretations of Islamic financial contracts, but according to Islamic jurisprudence all legitimate Islamic finance contracts should comply with the principles of Shariah. Therefore, in all Islamic contracts offered by Islamic banks and institutions there should be no form of *ribā*, no uncertainty, no investment in impermissible industries or products that do not comply with Shariah. However, although these principles are outlined by the Shariah in constituting what is compliant or not, there are some Islamic banks and institutions that may fall into dispute on individual contracts regarding its adherence to the Shariah. Some Islamic banks have their own interpretation of a contract and the acceptability of a contract is not always agreed upon. All Islamic banks and financial institutions have to refer to a Shariah Supervisory Board in determining the compliance of a contract in order to issue a transaction, which can be authorized as adhering to the principles of Islam.

There are three main categories of Islamic contracts that have been identified for the purpose of commercial and financial use: Islamic transactional contracts, exchange contracts and intermediation contracts, which are used significantly in commercial transactions and will be discussed individually in this chapter. Shariah compliant financial contracts aim to provide productive economic activity and social responsibility in adherence to key Islamic principles. The underlying principles of Shariah compliant finance involve rules such as that contracts cannot arouse debt, the payment of *ribā* is prohibited in all contracts, and there must be a risk sharing element involved between the two parties. In order for an Islamic contract to be valid there should also not be any uncertainty, to avoid potential disputes.

Any contract from an Islamic perspective could be viewed as being categorized into unilateral and bilateral contracts. Unilateral contracts include a transaction that benefits the customer or person receiving the fund, and bilateral contracts are consented by both parties who have signed the contract. There are also Islamic contracts that are not confined to being unilateral or bilateral, and these contracts are categorized on their validity to comply with the Shariah and their overall effect on the two parties. Islamic contracts can either be valid, void or voidable, and in order to be valid they have to adhere to the principles of Shariah. An Islamic contract becomes void if it goes against the major tenets of Islamic commercial law, e.g. if it includes *ribā* or uncertainty. An Islamic contract is voidable when the specified requirements of the contract are not fulfilled by one or both of the parties involved, and either one of the parties has to deliver the specified assets or service or withdraw from the contract. In many contracts there are cases when only one clause, which does not adhere to the Shariah, becomes void and the other clause remains valid.

Although there are many Islamic contracts and transactions which can be placed into different categories, the basic prerequisites of an Islamic contract involves a mutual agreement between two or more parties, an adherence to the principles of the Shariah, a capability to deliver the goods or asset and a specification of the desired product, service or investment. The most important aspect of any Islamic financial contract is that it does not contain any prohibited or contradictory terms which go against the rules of the Shariah or law in the respective country. Islamic financial contracts work well in providing an individual with the means to finance a transaction or manage their finances in adherence to their faith or through the desire of financing in an ethical manner compared to that of conventional financing. Conventional financing contracts are primarily based on interest, which can leave an investor or customer heavily in debt, as noted in the global economic crisis.

Many Islamic financial instruments are contracts which can assist in a transaction to the customer. Islamic finance and banking is formed on a set of contracts and instruments that provide the backbone of establishing ethical and socially responsible forms of investment, profit sharing and various other benefits for a person wanting to manage their finance in adherence to the Shariah and aim to promote its core values.

4.2 Transactional Contracts

Transactional contracts in Islamic finance and banking are based on the concept of sale and exchange or commodity trade based activities. These types of contracts create assets and include the exchange and sale of assets such as property, currency exchanges, and wealth or debt transfers. Another form of transactional contract is based upon partnership between two or more parties engaging in productive activities. This type of Islamic transactional contract relies upon the principle of profit and risk sharing. In these types of contract both parties can develop wealth by adhering to the sharing of risk. An example of an Islamic financial instrument that utilizes a transactional contract is *muḍārabah* and *mushārakah*. In addition, both of the parties could lose out if the investment does not gain profits. If we consider the *muḍārabah* contract, one party can provide capital to another party and this capital can be invested in a business or economic activity. Both parties in a *muḍārabah* contract have a partnership where they share the profits made from the investment based on a predetermined ratio, which has to be specified at the start of the initial contract. *Mushārakah* contracts are also considered to fall under the category of transactional contracts as *mushārakah* is based upon a joint venture partnership, where both parties are liable to provide the investment capital, expertise and talent for entrepreneurs, in addition to the labour. In the *mushārakah* contract both parties abide by the profit-and-loss sharing scheme as they have invested in the project on a joint basis.

Many Islamic transactional contracts are based on equity partnership. Equity-based partnership contracts in Islamic banking and finance include *murābaḥah*, *bay' bithaman 'ājil* and *tawarruq*. *Murābaḥah* is considered a transactional equity partnership contract as it operates as a cost plus sale transaction.

kinda
cut applies
in several
narrow
cases

Murābaḥah, an extremely popular contract that is offered by many Islamic banks and financial institutions worldwide, works through a financier who purchases a commodity in order to sell it to an entrepreneur or client with an agreed profit margin. The profit margin is most commonly referred to as a 'mark-up' when describing the process. An Islamic bank normally acquires the role of the financier and goes through a third party, such as the manufacturer of a product, from whom they purchase and then sell on to the buyer with a mark-up on the initial price of the commodity.

Bay' bithaman 'ājil is considered as a transactional Islamic financial contract as it also relies on the sale and purchase of an asset but works on a deferred payment scheme. This type of contract is not as transparent as the *murābaḥah* contract and there is some dispute as to whether it genuinely adheres to the principles of Shariah compliant financing. However, *bay' bithaman 'ājil* can still be categorized as a transactional contract due to the nature of the element of selling and purchasing involved in the contract.

Tawarruq is a form of reverse *murābaḥah*, which involves two transactions whereby a person purchases a commodity on a deferred payment basis and sells it at spot value, which means the payment has to be made on the spot but at a more reasonable and cheaper price than the original price. Many scholars disagree that *tawarruq* is Shariah compliant since there is an absence of economic activity that fulfils the principles of Shariah financing.

Many Islamic banks have also introduced consecutive partnership contracts, which enable depositors to be partners in a contract for a financial year and allows them to receive any profits made through the partnership during that period.[1] This type of partnership also constitutes being categorized as a transactional Islamic financial contract. There are many sectors

---

1.   M. B. Youssef, 'Islamic Financial Contracts', p. 2.

that can utilize Islamic transactional contracts, such as the real estate and infrastructure sectors or property development industries. Transactional contracts promote the creation of assets mostly through Shariah compliant economic activity, which can further spur investment opportunities for gaining profits.

There are challenges with transactional contracts, which are predominantly issues surrounding what is legitimately a Shariah compliant contract and what is not. The process of the sale and exchange of a commodity or the Islamic financial instrument used plays a crucial role and is the deciding factor on its authenticity or Shariah compliancy. All Islamic contracts which are categorized through transactional or partnership contracts have to adhere to the basic principles of the Shariah and this is significant in determining which contract to use when financing through an Islamic bank. Despite the disputes against certain Islamic financial instruments and contracts, which are not deemed to comply with the principles of the Shariah, there are some popular transactional contracts, which continue to be used *the whole kind for kind stuff.* by entrepreneurs, customers and businesses

4.3 Exchange Contracts

Islamic exchange contracts can predominantly be defined as sale contracts that enable the transfer of an asset or commodity in exchange for another commodity. In Islamic exchange contracts a client can transfer a commodity in exchange for a sum of money or transfer money in exchange for money such in the case of currency exchanges. Some popular Islamic exchange contracts include *murābaḥah*, since it operates as a cost plus contract. The *murābaḥah* contract enables an Islamic bank or financial institution to sell a commodity to a buyer for a price and also obtain a profit margin. Both the cost plus and the profit margin are pre-agreed by both parties, and this is mutually agreed and specified early on in the contract. The buyer is then liable to make deferred payments on the contract.

Another well-known exchange contract is the *salam*, which could also be defined as a forward contract whereby the customer purchases the commodity in full but it is delivered at a future specified date. An Islamic bank or financial institution is eligible to purchase the commodity on behalf of the customer, if needed, and this is where the exchange element occurs. Another type of forward sale contract, which can be categorized as an exchange 'contract, is *istiṣnā'*. This type of contract enables an Islamic bank or financial institution to purchase an investment project on behalf of the buyer. The project in *istiṣnā'* must fulfil the condition of economic activity or be under development with a guarantee of it being completed and delivered to the buyer on a specified date in the future.

There are many different types of exchange contracts in Islamic finance but the most popular involve the sale of goods, which can include a barter-style exchange of the goods or assets. An exchange contract in Islamic finance should hold some benefit to the individual or community if it is to adhere to the principles of Shariah compliant financing. There are some rules and regulations on exchange contracts that utilize Islamic financial instruments, such as the consensus that the price should be pre-agreed at the time of contracting the exchange transaction. It is advised that the ownership of any product, commodity or property should remain with the seller until the delivery of the completed project or product.

Bay' in Arabic means a transaction where the ownership of a commodity or asset is exchanged between the seller and the buyer in return for a profit. There are many Islamic financial instruments that adhere to the exchange of ownership in a Shariah compliant manner and often use *murābaḥah*. The seller and buyer can agree on the profit margin for the cost of the commodity being exchanged through a *bay'* exchange contract. A person wishing to enter a Shariah compliant exchange contract may not necessarily be in the position to offer a spot payment for the exchange of a commodity, and in this case there may be certain rules that apply under the Shariah. The prohibition of *ribā* is important when dealing with exchange contracts, especially in the case when an individual cannot afford to pay an instalment owed to the Islamic bank or institution. In the case of a default, assets may be taken in an exchange contract in order to ensure that negligence by a partner is dealt with without breaking the tenets of Shariah compliancy in financing.

The rules for exchange in Islamic finance and banking contracts and activities can be categorized into various types, such as on-the-spot exchange of goods or money, exchanges involving deferred payment, or spot delivery after the exchange is completed. For such exchange contracts there are certain rules that can be applied which differ from conventional exchange-based financial products. Conventional exchange-based contracts enable exchange transactions to be delayed and the commodity can be purchased by another party and sold without any liability of ownership. However, in an exchange contract from an Islamic bank or financial institution only one item from the exchange contract can be deferred and there is liability of ownership by the seller of the commodity.

Islamic exchange contracts differ considerably based upon the type of wealth or asset being sold and the various types of contracts that are made available from the Islamic bank or financial institution. When considering the types of exchange contracts and how they operate under Shariah compliant financing it is important to note that if there is an exchange in the form of a loan or a default in payment resulting in deferred payment there should be a guarantee of the full payment being made. Other exchange transactions, such as barter transactions, are quite rare in contemporary Islamic banking, and foreign exchange contracts are being developed in the Islamic banking sector.

4.4 Intermediation Contracts

Islamic financial intermediation contracts are based upon promoting the key concepts that govern Islamic finance and promote the core values of Shariah. An Islamic intermediation contract would normally utilize concepts such as risk sharing, fair and just transactions that are created with no exploitation for either party, real economic value of assets in a transaction, and avoidance of impermissible industries for investment or the financing of an industry that goes against the tenets of Islam. With these core values in mind, financial intermediation contracts can be further categorized into contracts that aid the safekeeping and security of an individual's funds. The main role of Islamic financial intermediation contracts is to help in facilitating transparency and effective use of some transactional contracts in adherence to the Shariah. Some Islamic intermediation contracts include *kifālah*, *ju'ālah*, *murābaḥah*, *amānah*, *takāful* and *wakālah*. For example, in a *kifālah* intermediation contract a third party becomes a guarantor for a debt to be cleared or an obligation to be fulfilled by another party. *Kifālah* is a promise given to the creditor, such as an Islamic bank or financial institution, that the debtor will indeed pay off the debt or fulfil any other financial obligation for which they are liable. This promise is outlined in the *kifālah* contract and the debtor is liable to be answerable to the creditor, which in this example is the Islamic Bank or financial institution. Under Islamic jurisprudence and Shariah law, the contract of *kifālah* ensures that the debtor is liable for the claim against them.

Ju'ālah is also considered to be an Islamic intermediation contract, which operates by offering a professional service for a pre-agreed sum or commission. In this contract one of the parties involved in a *ju'ālah* contract will pay another party an amount of money in order to utilize the professional services that they have outlined to be used in the contract. The *ju'ālah* contract relies upon specification of services in the contract to avoid any potential disputes and ensure that both parties are satisfied with the service delivered and the amount of commission paid. *Ju'ālah* contracts offer the option of utilizing a range of professional services, which include trust services, consultation or advice services for the betterment of society and in compliance with the societal benefits that Shariah finance promotes. *Ju'ālah* can be utilized in creating unique Shariah compliant financial structures; however the contract should specify the services that will be delivered as it is not a product that can be judged physically by an individual, rather it is a professional service of some sort that the individual will be either satisfied or dissatisfied with. This is why specification of the service is important when entering into the initial *ju'ālah* contract.

Muḍārabah is another popular Islamic financial contract, which facilitates financial intermediation due to the nature of the contract dealing with the partnership and trustee finance. *Muḍārabah* normally consists of a partnership between two parties, one party who provides the capital, such as the Islamic bank, and the other who has the expertise to carry out the service and use the capital for economic activity. Both partners will gain a share of the profits in this type of contract if the service renders well. Through the Islamic financial intermediation contracts of *kifālah*, *ju'ālah*, *amānah*, and *wakālah*, the services that can be utilized can expand to products that promote guarantees and insurance such as *Takāful* Islamic insurance. *Wakālah* is also considered to be an Islamic intermediation contract and operates through an agency contract whereby a fee may be paid to the agent for them to give representation of another person's interest. In addition, *amānah*, which are demand deposits, are a type of intermediation contract whereby deposits are held at an Islamic bank and the bank takes the role of keeping the deposits safely. The deposits made through *amānah* provide a guaranteed capital to the customer and do not profit or earn any returns.

There are some Islamic financial intermediation contracts that aim to aid transactional contracts such as *muḍārabah*, which constitutes a joint partnership venture and aids in the provision of capital by one partner for investment in a commercial enterprise or business. Islamic financial intermediation contracts are becoming increasingly popular and are offered in Islamic banks and Islamic financial institutions around the world to cater for the demand in facilitating and supporting specific projects, businesses and transactions. All Islamic financial instruments which are considered as intermediation contracts have to comply with the principles of the Shariah; they should not contain or promote *ribā*-based transactions or aid with any type of *ribā*. In addition, there should be transparency in all intermediation contracts which are utilized in order for the contracts to be deemed Shariah compliant and adhere to the principles of Islamic finance.

4.5 The Concept of *Wa'd* and *Mu'wada*

There are two significant concepts used in Islamic financial contracts: *wa'd*, which literally means unilateral promise in Arabic, and *mu'wada*, which means a bilateral promise. *Wa'd* constitutes a promise which is made by one person to another to undertake a certain actual or verbal commitment to another party, or a verbal proposition made by someone to undertake some action which will have benefit to the other person. For example, a person promises to sell their house to a friend. This is a unilateral, one-sided promise which only binds the person who has made the promise. According to the principles of Shariah, a promise should be kept as it promotes moral conduct and social responsibility. For the majority of Muslim jurists, fulfilling the *wa'd* is recommendable by the person who makes the promise. For other jurists, fulfilling the *wa'd* is obligatory except where justified. The Mālikī school of thought, however, sees the fulfilment of *wa'd* as obligatory, especially if the case presents problems for the unilateral promise.

Mu'wada constitutes a bilateral promise, when two parties implement two unilateral promises on the same subject. An example of a *mu'wada* is when a person promises to buy something from another person and the other person promises to sell something to that same person at the same fixed price. Many Islamic jurists do not agree with the concept of *mu'wada* as they argue that two unilateral contracts could result in a forward contract. There are two main schools of thought on the *mu'wada* promise, one which has been issued by the AAOIFI, Islamic Fiqh Academy and scholars, that it is only permissible when the bilateral promise is executed according to the Shariah, and the second from Ḥanafī scholars, who argue that forward contracts are permissible under the *mu'wada* principal as long as no other prohibitions are involved, such as uncertainty or short selling.[2]

The various schools of thought have different opinions on the use of both *wa'd* and *mu'wada*. Although promises are taken seriously in Islam and Islamic jurisprudence, nothing can constitute a legally binding Islamic financial contract in order to guarantee a level of security from both parties. Although some scholars argue that *wa'd* does constitute being legally binding

2.   Further reading in *Islamic Banker* on Islamic Contract Law retrieved from: http://www.ibdemo.org/education/islamic-contract-law.

without a written contract, many people can argue that there may be some room for uncertainty, which is prohibited in Islamic finance and banking. Although *wa 'd* is used between two parties it is more likely that an Islamic financial contract is utilized through an Islamic bank or financial institution.

4.6 Foreign Exchange and Islamic Contracts

Islamic finance has grown significantly throughout the years and is utilizing contemporary transactions in the increasingly popular foreign exchange (FX). The FX transaction works by providing an agreement of exchange of one currency for another at an agreed exchange rate. The agreement includes a specified date, to protect against unreasonable currency exchange rates, and aids in supporting businesses that operate in a foreign currency to establish exposure of risks. Foreign exchange hedging techniques may be used so that a business or enterprise can gain protection against negative currency exchanges set at a future date. The most popular type of FX transactions involve fund transfers from a variety of currencies in different countries, payment transactions, foreign currency fund transfers and remittances, investments, trading services and travellers cheques.

The general consensus amongst Islamic scholars regarding the use of FX is that currencies from various countries may be exchanged on the basis of an on-the-spot payment also known as a 'spot payment'. The exchange rate of the spot payment should be distinct, as different currencies from around the world hold different values both in their worth and power of purchase. The permissibility of currency exchange according to the principles of Shariah had opposing views in the past as many of the currency exchanges were based on forward contracts, when the rights or obligations of both parties involved are set to a date in the future.

The opposing views over whether currency exchange contracts are Shariah compliant arise due to the issue of existence of prohibited elements such as *ribā* and *gharar*, which constitutes excessive uncertainty. Another concern that Islamic scholars have with currency exchange contracts, in relation to Shariah compliant financing, is whether there would be the presence of speculation or gambling by either party.

For any FX transaction to be considered permissible, the uncertainty and speculation element needs to be considered. In a Shariah compliant transaction both futures and forwards involving the exchange of a currency is prohibited, since both forwards and futures involve the selling of a non-existent product or commodity that is not owned by the seller. Although there is a difference of opinion amongst Islamic scholars, who have argued that futures may be permissible if they have a valid cause – such as they could not meet delivery due to the current economic market and therefore the futures are inevitably bound to fail – this argument continues to be rejected by the consensus of scholars as they argue that under a futures contract both parties will be unable to deliver. Exchange rates in general are an unpredictable market and lack the basic Shariah compliant principle of being certain and transparent. Speculation is often rife regarding the future of exchange rates and could constitute impermissible methods of financing such as gambling, which go against the tenets of the Shariah.

In order for Islamic banks and financial institutions to deal with foreign exchange of currencies, they need to abide by an on-the-spot transaction process such as a bank transfer or remittance in a foreign currency. They can also deal with foreign currency payments for purchases of goods, which have been imported from another destination, and payment of services issued in a foreign currency. In addition, the selling and purchasing of a foreign currency by travellers cheques or bank drafts against a foreign currency are also accepted under spot transactions, where the payment is immediate. Islamic banks are eligible to obtain a profit margin on an FX transaction or a profit outlined in a contract. There are various Islamic hedging tools that can be utilized in the FX market, which have been developed with the aim of meeting the objectives of conventional currency hedging contracts whilst also maintaining Shariah compliancy. Therefore, any FX Islamic contract needs to ensure that it contains no interest, uncertainty or speculation.

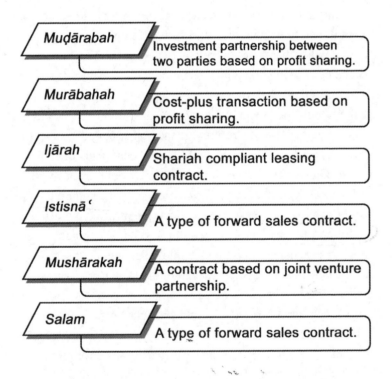

Figure 4.1: Categorization of Islamic Financial Contracts

Some Islamic FX exchange contracts involve forward contracts whereby one currency is sold on a set date against another currency whilst minimizing risks of differing exchange rates by predetermining the date that the transaction will take place. Future contracts can also be used as an agreement to buy and sell a currency for which it is delivered on a pre-agreed time scale, but according to Shariah futures are controversial due to the element of speculation. Foreign currency used as a hedging instrument can allow one currency to be exchanged to another currency at a specific time and a predetermined exchange rate, which should not change. In addition, Islamic FX exchange contracts can also utilize a swap contract, whereby an agreement is made for the exchange of one currency to another currency and then a reverse exchange is established for a future date.

ok so that is basically just a future.

which fucking different are he really drawing

squidgy

CHAPTER 5

Islamic Wealth Management

5.1 The Emergence of Islamic Wealth Management

The Islamic financial and banking industry has seen unprecedented growth and has provided an ethical alternative to conventional banking. It caters for the demands of both Muslims and non-Muslims who wish to utilize Shariah compliant ways of wealth management. The Islamic financial industry continues to be a rapidly advancing means of managing wealth and is set to grow in attracting investors from around the world due to the recognition that Islamic finance is receiving both in conventional Islamic hubs and the west.

Islamic wealth management is a sector of Islamic finance that has evolved significantly over the years. Several providers of Islamic financial products and services have now diversified their offerings beyond equities and real estate and there are currently a variety of Islamic wealth management structured products, multi-manager funds, *Takāful* and alternative investments available from major international, regional and national financial institutions around the world. Due to the growth of products, instruments and services that adhere to the principles of the Shariah there is an increasing need to utilize Islamic wealth management facilities.

Following the global financial crisis of 2007, financial institutions around the world fell heavily into debt. However, Islamic financial institutions and banks avoided being unduly affected by the financial crisis because of the ethical Shariah principle of the prohibition of *ribā*, which was one of the main causes that left conventional banks in debt. Islamic financial institutions have developed services for wealth management over the years, though previously there were no dedicated Islamic wealth management services and investors had to look to alternative services that may not have fully complied with the principles of the Shariah. The effects of the global financial crisis attracted interest in the Islamic finance industry as more investors looked for alternative ways of managing their wealth in an ethical manner, instead of using the conventional financial system.

According to Islamic principles, all wealth that an individual acquires derives and belongs to Allah, and the individual – based on the *amānah* (trust) concept – is responsible for managing their own wealth. Specifically, Islamic estate planning takes into consideration the concept and meaning of wealth in Islam, the religious requirements of making a will and the rules of inheritance. Social responsibility and accountability are deeply embedded in this concept. Wealth management, therefore, has three phases: first, the proper acquisition of wealth; secondly, the preservation of wealth; and third, the correct expenditure and distribution of wealth.[1]

---

1.   R. Boerner, M. Gassner and P. MacNamara, 'Wealth Management Cycle', p. 14.

Islamic estate planning predominantly manages the elements of preservation and distribution in managing wealth in a Shariah compliant manner. Islamic wealth management requires forward planning so that an individual can manage his or her wealth in accordance with the Shariah. A Muslim may follow Shariah principles in giving away their wealth to charity or family members after a death; however, they must acknowledge that the sole owner of any type of wealth is Allah (God). Many Islamic banks and financial institutions offer Islamic wealth management solutions to their customers and often refer to the SSB in advising on Shariah compliant wealth management products and instruments.

The management of assets and wealth in Islamic finance is very important, especially because the principles of the Shariah play a crucial role in adherence to the Islamic faith and is not solely a benchmark for managing finances. Conventional wealth management involves financial institutional investors such as insurance companies, pension funds, or lucrative corporations and individuals to invest in assets. Muslim investors used to turn to conventional financial institutions to have their assets managed with any returns from fixed-income securities given to charity or socially responsible fields to purify the returns. However, as the Islamic finance industry has grown significantly there are more Islamic financial institutions offering a range of products and services that are dedicated to managing assets in a Shariah compliant manner.

In managing wealth or assets there needs to be the presence of fund management options and discretionary portfolio services which satisfy the needs of the client. As there are an increasing number of Shariah compliant funds there are more opportunities for investors to utilize asset management services around the world. Clients who wish to utilize private banking institutions may want to use services such as management of trusts or inheritance-based services, and many private Islamic financial institutions can offer products to cater for these needs. In addition, there are a range of stocks, such as *ṣukūk* (Islamic bonds) and securities, which can aid in managing assets more effectively. In addition to Islamic financial institutions and banks there are many conventional banks that have also opened up specialized Islamic windows to cater for Islamic financial services, and many include windows for Islamic wealth management and asset management services.

5.2 Risks in Islamic Financial Products

In addition to the ordinary types of risks present in the conventional banking and finance industry, Islamic financial institutions also have Shariah compliance-related risks to consider based upon the financial products they offer. Many Islamic institutions and banks ensure that their Shariah complaint financial products adhere to the risks and returns being shared between a firm and its fund providers, whereas conventional financial institutions leave one party facing all of the risks and no risk for the fund providers. Theoretically, the risks involved in Islamic financial institutions and banks are lower than those of conventional institutions. However, Islamic banks and institutions share their own set of unique risks. Conventional banks and institutions are exposed to five categories of risks: credit risks, liquidity, reputation, operation and market risks. In order for any Islamic bank or finance institution to succeed in business they have to manage these risks in addition to a Shariah risk, which is unique to Islamic financial institutions.

Investors and stakeholders in Islamic financial institutions and banks acknowledge these risks and do their best to counteract these through the principles of Shariah. All Islamic financial institutions have individual aims to reduce risks and managing them to the best of their ability with each given transaction. There is a real need in Islamic financial contracts, products and transactions to be aware of the risks involved due to factors such as profit-and-loss sharing and Shariah compliancy, which are the two most important aspects of financial contracts in Islamic finance. The principles of Islamic finance ensure that there should be the sharing of both profits and losses in Islamic financial contracts and products such as saving accounts and investments. The sharing of risk is predominantly between the customer and the institution, or between two parties investing in a contract. In an Islamic bank, the customer enters into a contract aware that their investment will see a return only if the contract activity gains profits, and invests aware of the risks involved. The investment partner, such as the Islamic financial bank or institution, is expected to take precautions to reduce the risks as much as possible and ensure that any risks involved are disclosed and made transparent from the beginning of the contract.

Islamic financial institutions are not always able to mitigate their risks in comparison to conventional financial institutions. As there is a need for more options to be established to help Islamic firms mitigate their liquidity the Islamic capital market needs more development. Conventional capital markets have aided financial businesses to reduce their liquidity risks by offering them conventional interest-based financial instruments. However, Islamic financial institutions cannot use such instruments, which include *ribā* or any other form of derivatives, which go against the tenets of Islam in managing their risks. Therefore, Islamic capital markets need to seek ways of offering alternatives to managing risk in adherence to the Shariah and this is an area of Islamic banking and finance that needs more development.

In addition, many Islamic financial institutions do not have the same exposure to hedging techniques that are suitable to be used in Shariah compliant institutions. Islamic financial banks and institutions are continually developing innovative products and solutions for managing risk effectively, so that they can further excel in progressing the development and use of the growing Islamic finance and banking industry. Although there are risks involved in both Islamic and conventional financial institutions, Islamic finance has a relatively stable outlook in managing risks due to the ethical principles of the Shariah relating to real transactions in comparison to its conventional counterpart. In order for Islamic finance to reach its expected potential and fulfil industry growth and development worldwide it needs to focus on long term investments and how Islamic financial firms can manage risks involved in the long term. Safe commodity trading and the cost-plus sale of Islamic financing contracts that Islamic financial institutions and banks are offering have relatively less risks. This is significantly due to the nature of the prohibition of *ribā*, which has helped Islamic banks and institutions in offering ethical and socially responsible products and services to its clients.

5.3 Shariah Compliant Equities

Equity-based financing has played a significant role in facilitating the financing of trade and spurring on the financial industry over the years. With increasing development of enterprises and economic growth, equity-based financing continues to be a successful mode of financing due to there being less risks and more financial stability. In almost all Islamic finance contracts and transactions there is an element of risk involved. Although equity-based Shariah compliant instruments are generally more favourable for customers or clients, some Islamic banks and financial institutions try to offer Shariah compliant instruments which are based on equity investments. The two most popular Islamic financial contracts used for equity-based instruments in Islamic financial institutions are the *muḍārabah* partnership contract and the *mushārakah* joint venture partnership contract. The risks of equity investment arise due to the potential of a decrease in value of the equity, which is held by the Islamic financial institution or bank.

An Islamic financial institution or bank can participate in an equity-based investment, which can include investments in projects, joint ventures and Shariah compliant stocks. As all risks are shared between two or more parties in Islamic finance, there is the risk that if there is a default in the value of equity an investing company may lose any potential return on their investment and may also lose the capital invested. The institution or bank can try to reduce associated equity risks by considering factors such as an efficient business plan from the managing partner, the economic environment in which the project will occur and whether there may be any potential legal issues in the investment. These factors should be considered by the Islamic bank or financial institution before entering into any equity-based contract with another party or firm. If these factors are not considered then the Islamic bank or institution may be exposed to risks involving credit and liquidity. In addition, Islamic banks and institutions would benefit from overseeing the investment following the signing of the contracts, to ensure that risks are reduced in all stages of the process.

There has been an increase in equity financial firms around the world, including stock markets which run organized exchanges, and these have become a significant part of financial intermediation and focusing on savings for long term investments. Risk sharing, which is a key principle in Islamic financial contracts, is an aspect that is implemented by investors in the stock markets. Conventional stock markets generally offer liquidity for listed shares but also carry the risks of a crash in the stock market, which can significantly affect those saving, or pension funds. The market can be volatile, and conventional financial stock markets can be exposed to challenges where investors may lose more money, especially if they experience a market crash in stocks.

The development of Shariah compliant stocks and equity-based financing could pave the way for other countries to utilize an alternative to the interest-based conventional financial system. The development of long term equity-based banking services and products and efficient Shariah compliant stock markets could provide a lucrative alternative for economic growth around the world. Developing countries could benefit from Shariah compliant stock markets, which can spur financial growth and create additional employment, and drive a country's economy forward. One advantage of Islamic financial contracts is that there are many equity-based contracts such as *muḍārabah*, which can help when sharing the profits and losses. This enables both parties to be responsible for the investment and the sharing of profits and any losses incurred will be shared by both parties.

Many investors and enterprises would prefer to deal with equity-based financial products or contracts, as they have recognized the scope for significant returns and profits in investing their wealth this way. There has been a predominant demand for indices, which have been displayed through Dow Jones Indexes, the FTSE Group, Morgan Stanley Capital International (MSCI) and Standard & Poors (S&P), who all offer services for equities. The Global Dow Jones Index, for example, has satisfied Shariah compliant equity investing as long as the investment is permissible and in accordance to the principles of Islam. Investing in Shariah compliant stocks that adhere to the principles of Islam is becoming increasingly popular, with the development of new innovative products and services which cater for increasing economic growth and enhancing the economy.

Islamic banking has proven to be socially equitable due to the nature of no-interest based transactions and more stability in sharing risks between the two parties.

The ethical principles of profit-and-loss sharing, the risks being carried between two or more parties, and other key factors based upon financing in accordance with the Shariah has made equity-based financing an attractive option for investors and individuals wishing to utilize Shariah compliant products and services.

5.4 The Outlook for Islamic Wealth Management

Islamic wealth management is a sector of Islamic finance that has evolved significantly over the years and continues to leave room for development of innovative Shariah compliant solutions. Several providers of Islamic financial products and services have now diversified their offerings beyond equities and real estate in the Islamic wealth management sector. There is currently a variety of Islamic wealth management structured products, multi-manager funds, *Takāful* and alternative investments available from major international, regional and national financial institutions around the world. Due to the growth of products, instruments and services that adhere to the principles of the Shariah there is more of a need to utilize Islamic wealth management facilities and contracts based upon the tenets of Islam. Risk sharing is a predominant factor in Islamic financial transactions and contracts, and it has been shown to be inherently more stable and socially equitable in the management of wealth. As risks are shared in Islamic finance contracts, investors can be reassured that credit cannot expand in comparison to conventional institutions.

The development of Islamic wealth management can be nurtured by raising awareness of the benefits of the risk sharing system and dispelling the myths surrounding equity-based Shariah compliant financing. In addition, reducing the costs of Shariah compliant transactions in the stock markets can further help to attract more ethical means of wealth management. Developing more long term Islamic financing instruments and low cost secondary markets for equity-based trading can assist in developing Islamic wealth management solutions. Secondary markets for trading stocks at a lower price could create an expanded distribution of risk and therefore succeed in reducing risk, with potential returns that could be lucrative for investors.

Both market participants and investors can benefit from relatively lower risks when managing their wealth in a Shariah compliant manner in comparison to conventional financing, which is exposed to risk of *ribā* and other prohibited elements. Conventional financial institutions operate in establishing a sound understanding of the client's needs and what they want to achieve from their investments and developing strategies to meet these requests. In the same way, Islamic financial institutions can adopt the interest of meeting their clients' needs and understanding their aims so that they can offer effective strategies and find ways to reduce risks. A choice of investments in an Islamic bank or financial institution will be offered to clients to provide effective solutions, and more products and services are being developed to cater for the demand in Shariah compliant investments.

Wealth and asset management in Islamic finance is an industry that needs to be developed in order to spur further growth in Islamic banking and financial products, services and investments in the long term. Islamic wealth management solutions are developing steadily, but the industry needs a significant increase in profitability and sales volumes to see a major development and rise in profits. Islamic financial institutions can further develop wealth and asset management products so that investors or clients can utilize Islamic financial instruments to facilitate their individual requirements. Many Islamic banks and financial institutions choose to use a mixture of funds and investments in order to meet their client's objectives and these instruments differ significantly from their conventional counterparts.

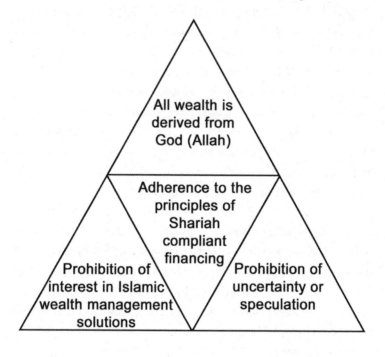

Figure 5.1: Principles Underlying Islamic Wealth Management

An important element of Islamic wealth management is to reduce risk when making transactions or potential investments in a Shariah compliant manner. It is inevitable that risks will increase over a longer period of time, however many industry experts believe that long term investments have a higher chance of profitability than short term investments, which is why the Islamic finance industry needs to direct their attention to long term investment solutions for managing wealth. Liquidity is a challenge for both the Islamic finance industry and the conventional financial industry alike. Secondary markets have addressed these challenges and the liquidity of equity shares has been taken into account. The 'over the counter' trade scheme enables deposits that are held in investment accounts at an Islamic bank or financial institution to be transferred to another owner. An organized stock market for exchanges where listed shares are traded at a lower price can also aid in developing liquid markets for Islamic financial investments.

The wealth management sector is important to the Islamic finance and banking industry and continues to be a rapidly advancing means of managing finances. The Islamic finance industry is set to grow in attracting investors from around the world, which is becoming increasingly aware of the benefits of Islamic wealth and asset management in comparison to conventional wealth management solutions.

CHAPTER 6

Islamic Investments

Islamic investments are based upon the tenets of Islam and are a unique form of ethical and socially responsible investing in beneficial sectors, which can spur and nurture economic growth. Islamic investments are investments that comply with the principles of Islamic law and all potential investments need to be authorized by an SSB. Most Islamic banks and institutions have established an investment policy for Shariah compliant investments, which are dedicated to either institutional or individual investors. The SSB, which consists of a group of Islamic scholars or jurists, considers each potential investment product or service that is presented to them to confirm whether the products are compliant with Islamic law and jurisprudence. The main route in establishing Shariah compliancy of an investment is firstly taken from the Qur'an and then the Sunnah. In addition, the SSB will consider teachings from the Prophet's companions and their actions, scholarly legal deductions and come to an overall consensus on the potential investment product, contract or service.

Due to the ethical principles of Shariah compliant financing the global economic financial crisis did not affect the Islamic banking industry profoundly, and Islamic investments fared better than other conventional investments, especially because of the nature of the absence of risk in investment, transaction or contract. Investors from around the world were attracted to the benefits that Islamic banking and financial investments could bring to the table and global investors and financial institutions are looking at Shariah compliant investments and their potential for global expansion with new interest.

Islamic financial institutions establish an Islamic investment policy for the institutional or individual investor, and the creation of Islamic investment products present their own unique challenges. In adherence to the principles of the Shariah, all parties entering into a contract or investment need to have full transparency of the specifications of the investment and the amount of profits or share that they are entitled to prior to signing the contract. Transparency of the challenges and risks involved should be disclosed with all transactions or contracts issued by an Islamic bank or institution, and the process for the investment policy begins with the SSB. The existence of the SSB sets Islamic investments apart from conventional investments, and Shariah scholars on the board not only authorize Shariah compliant investments but also oversee that the investment remains Shariah compliant throughout the process.

Still evolving, the ethical principles of the Islamic investment sector has created a socio-economic component that is attractive to people of all faiths, not just Muslims alone. There are, however, aspects of an Islamic investment that need to be considered. For example, if the investment does not involve any tangible items it may be impermissible and therefore should be avoided by all parties, including the Islamic financial institution. The prohibition of gambling investments is also taken very seriously, as any investment involving risks of games involving chance – such as casinos or investments that generate derivatives – are considered impermissible in Islamic finance investments. The main principle, which needs to be implemented in all Islamic investments, is the prohibition of *ribā*, which means in compliance with the Shariah any investment which generates a form of interest must be avoided.

The Islamic investment sector has more opportunities for growth due to the ethical principles of Islamic finance and the promotion of socially responsible investing. One sector which may need to be developed in relation to Islamic investments is the corporate finance sector, as it is significantly reliant upon interest-bearing instruments, especially in the conventional financial industry. As usury and interest (*ribā*) is prohibited in Islamic finance, the application of Islamic law in handling corporate finance exposes new challenges, including the feasibility of the portfolio manager, which would need to be invested in, and the adherence to the principles of the Shariah when managing stocks, as corporate finance may put pressure on companies to borrow and use interest. Both Islamic and conventional financial institutions face the same issues, such as how to develop investment products and monitor policies according to their respective client's objectives and specific requirements. The lack of standardization of Shariah compliancy of products around the Muslim world may cause challenges to the Islamic investment sector and there is a real need for harmonization of industry practices.

As the Islamic finance and banking industry continues to grow there is more scope for Shariah compliant investment products and services to pave the way for ethical investments that can better the society at large. Islamic financial investments should promote sound ethics and financial products that do not exploit one or more of the participating investors in any transaction. Due to the expanding range of Islamic financial products and instruments there is more scope for investments that can utilize these products, across a variety of different sectors within the industry. Investment projects that comply with the principles of the Shariah and promote the core values of Islamic financing can further spur socially responsible facilities and create a more stable economy, especially in developing countries around the world. With the growth of more products and financial instruments that Islamic financial institutions can offer there is greater scope for investments in Shariah compliant industries such as *ṣukūk* Islamic bonds or *Takāful* Islamic insurance products, which have a growing market around the world.

6.1 The System for Islamic Investments

The system for Islamic investments is predominantly governed by the principles of Shariah rulings, which govern all investment projects and contracts. The first aspect of any investment is that it should adhere to the prohibition of *ribā*, uncertainty, and speculation, which are the underlying features of all Islamic business transactions. Any portfolio for investment should contain a detailed Islamic investment management vehicle, which is managed by an Islamic financial institution or bank. Investment management vehicles should include a specific Shariah compliant investment strategy and processes that involve focusing on deal-screening criteria,[1] investment processes, the structure of the investment vehicle or instrument and the investment constraints which need to be addressed. In a Shariah compliant investment there should be a deal-monitoring criteria to recognize due diligence procedures, especially in private Shariah compliant

---

1.   O. Ahmed, 'Islamic Investing: An Institutional Investors Perspective', p. 137.

equity-based investments. Each equity-based investment would need to exhibit a sound and efficient business model and have an organized team overseeing the management of the potential investment. The objectives of a Shariah compliant investment should not engage in unlawful business and this should be established from the very beginning, as well as due diligence prior to an investment.

The main structure of an investment vehicle used in making Shariah compliant investments should be predominantly based on equity. According to Islamic law, the most desirable structure for an Islamic investment vehicle is one that is based on partnerships. It is imperative for the implementation of an Islamic investment to be based upon the vehicle of profit-and-loss sharing and avoid any *ribā*-based transactions. Lastly, the investment strategy involved in making Islamic investments involves the actual constraints on the investment. There should not be more than 10 per cent of funds invested in a single company. In addition, investments should contain trade or lease-financing opportunities and adhere to the principles of Islam.

Many Shariah compliant investments are based on the equity, which is an ordinary share given to a shareholder with specific rights of ownership over the assets of a company. In the equity-based investment system, profits and losses have to be shared in any venture. In conventional investments an investor may not follow the profit-and-loss sharing scheme and therefore more risks will be placed on one party in relation to the other. In equity-based Shariah compliant investments the process ensures that the most that an investor can lose is the principle amount that they had invested, but not any excess amount of funds, in comparison to conventional investments whereby an investor can lose in excess funds too, based on interest. An Islamic investment in the shares of a company requires compliancy with the Shariah, and the equity-based system of making Shariah compliant investments share the risks between two or more parties enables a more ethical approach to making investments.

Another method of investing in Islamic finance is trading in a Shariah compliant manner. Trading has becoming an increasingly popular sector for investors, especially those who use conventional financial institutions, and the mechanism of trading and investing operates on the trading of commodities, shares and foreign currencies. Many brokers traditionally used to offer a service to conventional investors to pay cash to the brokers account and in return the investor would be issued with a share certificate. Nowadays, a contract for differences (CFD) is issued and this operates where the investor bets on the price of the share or commodity of foreign currency, which constitutes gambling. Gambling is an industry that does not comply with the principles of Shariah and it is prohibited to make an investment through gambling or betting by chance on the outcome of shares. Instead, investors wishing to make trading investments in a Shariah compliant manner need to ensure that there is the existence of an underlying asset.

There are many factors that need to be considered when making Shariah compliant investments. An investor needs to consider the subject of the investment and its adherence to the Shariah, the instruments used to facilitate the investment and the institution used, such as an Islamic bank or Islamic financial institution. These institutions have to refer to a Shariah Supervisory Board to ensure that all investments are fully Shariah compliant, so that the investor has the reassurance that they are investing in an ethical manner. There are many entrepreneurs who wish to make a Shariah compliant investments through an Islamic financial institution or bank. An entrepreneur can make an investment in a social enterprise through an Islamic financial institution, who can act as another party to invest in the enterprise under a pre-agreed share of profits and losses.

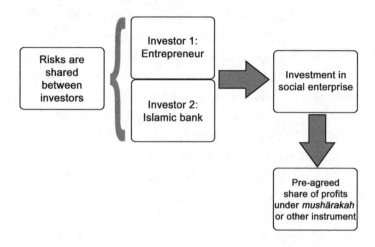

Figure 6.1: A System of Islamic Investments

The entrepreneur can manage the investment with their business goals and expertise and the institutional investor can also invest in the enterprise through an Islamic bank instrument such as *mushārakah*, where losses are shared in proportion to the capital contributed by each party. As with any contract there are considerable risks, however this ethical system is a justified method of making investments through Islamic banks or financial institutions. The operational process of making an investment in a social enterprise through an Islamic bank or financial institution is shown in Figure 6.1. An investor must take many considerations into account in the processes and methods of facilitating an Islamic investment, but the underlying principles of Islamic finance can have many benefits for investors wishing to profit from a Shariah compliant investment. Having a sound business plan and outlining strategies for a potential investment can further spur lucrative profitability and ensure that sound investments are made to compound economic growth and deliver beneficial facilities to society at large.

6.2 Shariah Compliant Sectors for Investments

Islamic finance offers a variety of lucrative and ethical sectors for investors, which can aid in spurring economic growth and promote socially responsible investing in areas that can further benefit society whilst still adhering to the principles outlined by the Shariah. Some of the key investment sectors in Islamic finance that investors are tapping into are the areas of *ṣukūk* (Islamic bonds), *Takāful* (Islamic insurance), real estate and infrastructure, as outlined in Figure 6.2. There may be more Shariah compliant sectors for investments that are developing as the industry grows, such as Islamic microfinance and energy and resources. Many Islamic financial institutions have opened up specialised businesses for *Takāful* services and many Islamic banks and financial institutions are aiding with the issuance of *ṣukūk* bonds as an alternative to conventional bonds. *Ṣukūk* can be implemented into many other areas of investment sectors such as real estate and infrastructure sectors.

The real estate sector is also proving successful in spurring economic activity for Islamic investments. Investing in real estate and properties is a recommended form of investment under the tenets of Islamic financing. Properties can obtain profits from rental income, in addition to capital gain. There are two main types of investment properties that an investor can consider, such as a commercial and residential property, although commercial property under Shariah finance may have some legal complexities and a lawyer may be needed to oversee matters pertaining to maintenance and leasing under Shariah compliant financial instruments. Under Islamic finance rulings, if an investor does not have sufficient money to invest in the purchase of a property on their own they may wish to partner with other investors and form a joint ownership contract. The real estate sector can be a profitable avenue to spur capital gains in the long term.

Infrastructure is another key sector for Islamic financial investments, if structured properly. Islamic finance offers a wide range of products and financial instruments to aid in project financing, including the ability to issue *ṣukūk* for large scale infrastructure investments. In addition, Islamic financial investors can benefit from the flexibility of *ṣukūk* on a standalone basis for infrastructure projects. The sector has the potential to utilize Islamic financial investments in funding infrastructure development, especially in emerging economies. The asset-backing element of Islamic financing, which is a governing principle in any investment, makes it better suited to infrastructure-based projects in comparison to conventional financial methods. A typical trait of infrastructure-based investments is that investors prefer longer tenures, which can be utilized in *ṣukūk* to fund long term infrastructure projects. There are many benefits of investing in the infrastructure sector as it can spur room for employment, housing and has many socio-economic benefits, especially if the investment is made in developing countries around the world.

Another area for Shariah compliant investments is in specific commodities. Many investors choose to buy commodities in order to benefit from a future rise in profits under conventional schemes. However, some of these investments do not fall under Shariah compliancy and are prohibited according to the principles of Shariah such as alcohol, pork, pornography and weapons. Profits obtained by investing in companies which partially engage in such industries can be purified by donating some portion of the profit to charities. This is allowed by Shariah scholars only if the profits of the companies do not exceed 5 per cent and their main income comes from permitted activities. There are also various Shariah compliant indexes that can be invested in, such as the Dubai Shariah Hedge Fund Index, FTSE Shariah Global Equity Index, Dow Jones Islamic Market Index, and Indonesia Shariah Stock Index.

The various sectors for investment that remain to be Shariah compliant are wide and varied. As more Islamic financial institutions and banks implement new innovative Shariah compliant products and services, there is more scope for investors to make sound investments. Any investor considering the various sectors should ensure that the sector they are wishing to invest in is one that complies with the Shariah and does not go against the tenets of Islam. This is a very important aspect governing all investments and any potential sector in which an investor wishes to utilize their funds should adhere to this principle.

The positive developments in the Islamic banking and finance industry are attracting attention worldwide and can only further help in the establishment of Islamic investments. Islamic financial markets now offer nearly all the products and services that conventional markets are offering apart from those that do not abide by the Shariah. Products such as money market and capital market instruments have been developed by Islamic financial institutions in order to cater for Islamic investments. These products not only cater to investors who are looking for Shariah compliant investments but acts as a Shariah compliant funding avenue for the expansion of businesses and their services. The various sectors that are outlined in Figure 6.2 are some of the key sectors for Islamic investors to consider, however there are many other growing sectors, such as the Islamic microfinance industry, that are also providing opportunities for investment. Islamic microfinance investments have helped developing countries to gain funds for projects involving education, health and medicine, and services for those in need, and is a sector that may see a rise as more products and services are being developed. Investments that promote the core values of Islamic finance and further aid in developing funds that provide social or economic stability are looked upon with great respect in the Islamic finance industry.

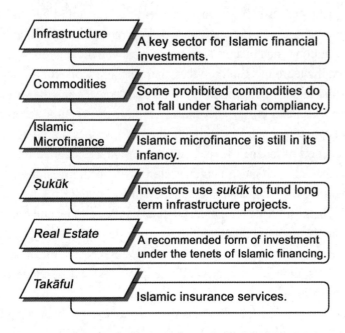

Figure 6.2: Sectors for Islamic Investment

CHAPTER 7

Ṣukūk

The history of the *ṣukūk* market has been shaped by the development of an international and globally renowned Islamic 'bond'. Due to the progress in the establishment of Islamic financial instruments worldwide to cater for the growing demands of investor needs, the sector is set to further grow and prosper. The concept of Islamic bonds were generally unheard of in traditional Islamic financing, and many scholars would deem it impermissible due to the nature of its issuance, especially as it involves prohibitive elements.

The *ṣukūk* market is now a global Islamic financial sector, which is not only appealing to the Muslim world but also to the west. In December 2001,[1] Malaysian business Kumpulan Guthrie Berhad was unprecedented in issuing the first international *ṣukūk*, which paved the way for further *ṣukūk* issuances. The Malaysian *ṣukūk* was a US dollar denominated *ṣukūk*, which aimed to attract

---

1. R. Wedderburn-Day, 'Sovereign SUKUK: Adaptation and Innovation', p. 325.

investors and entrepreneurs from Asia and the Middle East. A year later, in July 2002,[2] the Federation of Malaysia issued a second *ṣukūk*, which was again US dollar denominated. For the first time, Malaysia achieved an international credit rating for its first *ṣukūk* issuance and this further spurred interest in other countries to issue *ṣukūk*s. The sector has grown significantly since then and *ṣukūk*s have been issued worldwide; in Asia, the Middle East, Europe and America. *Ṣukūk* issuances are still dominant in Malaysia and the GCC region, which are financial hubs for Islamic finance and banking instruments, and other countries which have tapped into the *ṣukūk* sector are Bahrain, Qatar, Saudi Arabia, Kuwait, Oman, UAE, Germany, Pakistan, Indonesia, UK and the US to name but a few.

Traditionally *ṣukūk* was not considered a Shariah compliant sector due to the nature of the system of conventional bonds and the structure of these types of bonds, which would have had to change if it were to be developed into a Shariah compliant alternative. However, since the global economic crisis of 2007, the Islamic finance industry was propelled into the spotlight and many Islamic scholars began to accept *ṣukūk* issuances. By the end of 2007, the *ṣukūk* industry had grown significantly, showing lucrative profits for investors both from the Muslim world and internationally. The International Monetary Fund issued a report in July 2008 outlining the rapid growth in issuances around the world and the Accounting and Auditing Organisation for Islamic Financial Institutions (AAOIFI) issued their own statement on *ṣukūk* and their responsibility towards arranging or issuing a *ṣukūk* in line with the Shariah. AAOIFI advise Islamic financial institutions to adhere to ensuring that a number of requirements are met when issuing *ṣukūk*, such as ensuring that the *ṣukūk* is tradable and owned by the *ṣukūk* owners.

---

2.   Ibid., p. 326.

The growing acceptance of *ṣukūk* from Islamic scholars and economists instilled trust in the product and this was reflected in its rapid growth and in issuances from around the world. In 2008, the growth of *ṣukūk* was rising, and surged within the first ten months, and was rapidly developing to incorporate Shariah compliant structures to be used in product issuances. This resulted in a fall in the number of issuances in order to comply with the principles of the Shariah, although *ṣukūk* issuances that used the *ijārah* sale and leasing structure were not affected and were most sought after by sovereign issuers worldwide. The western world began to see the significant benefits that *ṣukūk* could bring to their respective economies, but due to the global economic crisis there was a delay in issuances – especially from the UK government who launched its first ever *ṣukūk* issuance in 2015. The Islamic principles of the prohibition of interest, which governs all *ṣukūk* issuances and other Islamic financial instruments, would need to be adhered to in issuing any type of *ṣukūk*. The UK issued a short-term *ṣukūk* using an *ijārah*-based structure. However, there were a number of challenges that needed to be overcome in order to structure an efficient *ṣukūk*, such as regulation and taxation issues. Since 2008, the UK placed *ṣukūk* on hold, but in October 2013, the British prime minister, David Cameron, announced his plans to issue the first ever UK *ṣukūk* at the World Islamic Economic Forum in London.

The growing interest in *ṣukūk* is due to the rise and benefits of the absence of *ribā* in all *ṣukūk* issuances, which enables investors to deal with bonds without using interest and falling into debt. Many conventional bonds may have additional risks whereby interest is used, and investors may lose more than they originally invested due to the existence of interest-based transactions. On the other hand, *ṣukūk* also faces equity and Shariah-based risks, which makes a distinction between the two products. There are a growing number of countries around the world that have expressed an interest in the lucrative ṣukūk sector and it is continuing to be a highly popular Islamic financial instrument for investors and companies alike. There have been some major ṣukūk issuances around the world that will be further discussed in the subsequent sections of this chapter, which reflect the diversity and popularity of the Islamic bond. There are different types of ṣukūk available and an investor can benefit from choosing the right structure and instrument according to their respective investments. Many Islamic financial institutions offer instruments to aid in ṣukūk issuances such as the *ijārah* leasing structured instrument, which is the most popular form used in ṣukūk issuances around the world.

7.1 What is Ṣukūk?

Ṣukūk is the Arabic term for bond and refers to the Shariah compliant equivalent to bonds. The word ṣukūk derives from the issuance of papers that were used to represent commodities for payments of salary in the early Islamic period, and this was often referred to as '*suk*'. In contemporary times ṣukūk has been used to issue certificates, which represent the shares in ownership of usufruct of an asset or tangible assets. Ṣukūk differs from conventional bonds, which are confined to the ownership of a debt, by enabling investors to have a share of an asset and in addition gain from commensurate cash flow and shared risks.

Any ṣukūk issuance has to adhere to the principles of the Shariah and ensure that all issuances do not involve any *ribā*, *gharar* and investment in prohibitive activities or commodities. The Islamic capital markets have developed significantly since the establishment of the ṣukūk in recent years. Islamic financial instruments can aid with the facilitation of a ṣukūk issuance

and the actual *ṣukūk* can create a link between issuers, such as
sovereigns and businesses, with investors who want to diversify
their holdings. There are an increasing number of *ṣukūk* issuances
in major Islamic financial hubs such as the Middle East and
Asia, and *ṣukūk* is growing and developing in other countries
around the world – including major financial centres such as
the UK. Any funds raised from a *ṣukūk* issuance are expected
to adhere to the principles of Islamic commercial law and be
used in permissible industries or projects. Most funds acquired
through a *ṣukūk* issuance are used in transparent ways, such as
for infrastructure development, education establishments or any
other socially responsible project, which respond to the needs of
the real economy.

Most *ṣukūk* issuances have to be approved by a Sharia
Supervisory Board, and it is compulsory that both domestic
and foreign investors consult a SSB on the legitimacy of the
issuance and the structure they intend to use to facilitate the
ṣukūk issuance in their respective country. The issuance of *ṣukūk*
has exhibited resilience, especially following the global financial
crisis, and the market has since grown to extend offerings to
international capital markets. Although the *ṣukūk* market is still
relatively a niche sector, it has huge potential for development
and growth around the world and many western countries are
tapping into *ṣukūk* bonds that are proving to be more beneficial
than conventional bonds.

Many people have found the concept of Shariah compliant
bonds difficult to understand since the principle system of
conventional bonds does not comply with the financial system
of the Shariah. However, *ṣukūk* bonds, which are structured
by using Islamic financial instruments, provide an alternative
way for promoting developmentalism, which considers the
environment. As most Islamic finance and banking transactions
and investments are based upon ethical considerations there

is scope to attract the conventional investor in participating in highly ethical ways of financing.

7.2 How does *Ṣukūk* work?

Ṣukūk is an Islamic bond that can be categorized as having three main purposes: for project specific funds, asset specific funds and balance sheet funds. In a project-based fund, all of the money that the *ṣukūk* raises is used towards a specific investment project, such as for an infrastructure development or construction. In the case of the funds being utilized for asset specific purposes, the *ṣukūk* funds are used in mobilizing resources so that it can be used to sell off the beneficiary right of the assets to the investors. An example of an asset-based *ṣukūk* would be the funding of a hospital, and the underlying asset would be the land used for the construction of the hospital, which is sold to the investor. Lastly, *ṣukūk* can be used for balance sheet specific purposes, which may be more significantly used by Islamic banks or financial institutions. *Ṣukūk* utilized for a balance sheet purpose works by mobilizing funds to be used on a variety of different investment projects and is primarily used by Islamic financial institutions which need to use the funds for more than one project.

There are many types of *ṣukūk* available, and these types are categorized by their individual structuring and the Islamic financial instrument or contract used to facilitate the *ṣukūk*. The AAOIFI has outlined specific standards for the types of *ṣukūk* and set fourteen standards for *ṣukūk* issuances. The main forms of *ṣukūk* are known to be the *ijārah*, *muḍārabah*, *mushārakah*, *istiṣnāʿ*, and *murābaḥah* and hybrid forms of *ṣukūk*.

The *muḍārabah ṣukūk* (shown in Figure 7.1) is predominantly based upon investments that represent the ownership of units of equal value, which are registered through a *muḍārabah* equity.

Muḍārabah ṣukūk holders are considered the suppliers of capital, better known as *rab al-māl*, and own the shares of *muḍārabah* equity, and returns on the shares are given according to their individual percentage of ownership. *Muḍārabah ṣukūk* holders are eligible to transfer their ownership by selling the deeds of *ṣukūk* through the securities market. *Muḍārabah ṣukūk* are used to encourage investors from the public to participate in larger based investment projects. The holders become silent partners who do not play an active role in managing any underlying assets of the investment project, and the working partner involved in the *ṣukūk* is under the obligation to oversee the management and provide the working capital. The *ṣukūk* working partner is entitled to a share of the profit, which is normally decided upon signing the contract with an investor under the *muḍārabah* structure. The *muḍārabah ṣukūk* could be summed up as being a *ṣukūk* issuance that is based upon an equity partnership between two or more parties.

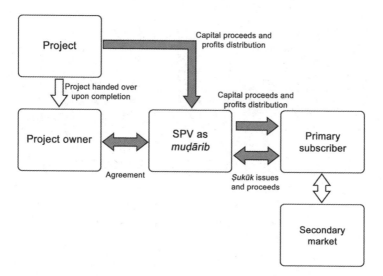

Figure 7.1: The *Muḍārabah Ṣukūk* Structure

The *mushārakah ṣukūk* is predominantly based on a joint venture partnership that is normally equity-based and works similar to a *muḍārabah ṣukūk*. *Mushārakah ṣukūk* is primarily used for establishing a new or existing investment project through a joint partnership contract, which adheres to the principles of the Shariah. The holders of a *mushārakah ṣukūk* certificate take ownership of the investment project or asset according to their respective shares in the *ṣukūk* investment. The *mushārakah ṣukūk* operates when an obligator/originator of *ṣukūk* signs the contract with an investor that declares a profit sharing percentage and outlines the transfer of business or assets that the obligator in the contract has to give as part of the joint venture partnership.

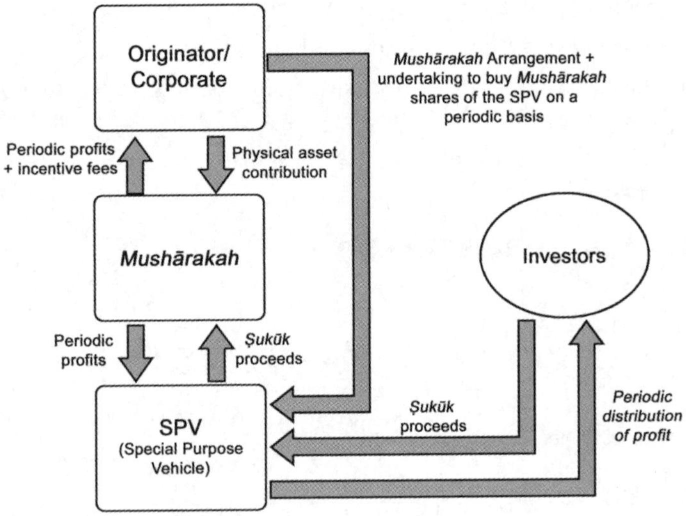

Figure 7.2: The *Mushārakah Ṣukūk* Structure

The *ijārah ṣukūk* is considered to be the most popular type of *ṣukūk* both in the Muslim world and the west and is predominantly based upon the leasing or rental contract. An *ijārah ṣukūk* works by leasing an asset for a fee and the investor can take ownership of the asset through the *ṣukūk* issuance and will receive a return when the asset is leased out representing the equal shares given to investors who have ownership of an asset. This type of *ṣukūk* is more likely to be used in the scenario of rented real estate, usufruct of a real estate, or infrastructure development as presented in Figure 7.3.

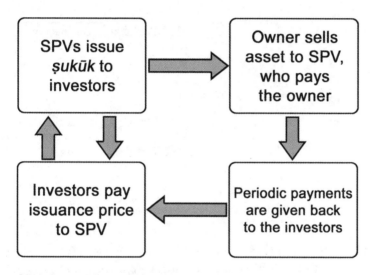

SPV: Special Purpose Vehicle

Figure 7.3: The *Ijārah Ṣukūk* Contract

Murābaḥah ṣukūk is based on a cost sale deferred payment contract and operates as an agreement between an investor and seller for an asset. *Ṣukūk* based upon the *murābaḥah* contract involves the SPV (special purpose vehicle) who can utilize the investor's capital in purchasing and selling an asset to the buyer on a cost plus profit basis. In return the buyer is eligible to make deferred payments to the investor who is selling the asset. The income derived from the *murābaḥah ṣukūk* is predetermined and fixed, as outlined in the contract, and the SPV aids in facilitating transactions between the holders of the *ṣukūk* and the buyers.

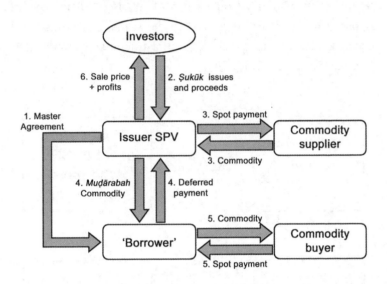

Figure 7.4: The *Murābaḥah Ṣukūk* Structure

The *istiṣnā' ṣukūk* works as a Shariah compliant project-based bond. In this type of *ṣukūk* two parties are involved, such as the buyer and the manufacturer. The holders of an *istiṣnā' ṣukūk* are considered the buyers and the manufacturer/contractor is the obligator, who delivers the project or asset at a predetermined date in the future. The holder of an *istiṣnā' ṣukūk* can lease the asset to another party under the *ijārah* contract and gain from regular payments. The working mechanism of an *istiṣnā' ṣukūk* is summarized in Figure 7.5.

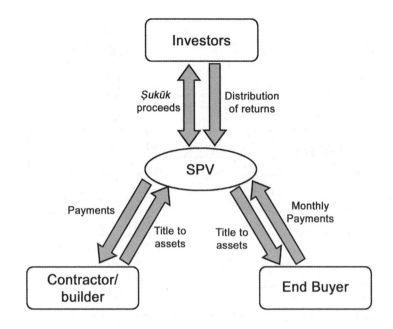

Figure 7.5: The *Istiṣnāʿ Ṣukūk* Structure

Lastly, in the *salam*-based *ṣukūk*, which is also known as a deferred delivery purchase *ṣukūk*, the holders of the *ṣukūk*, which are the investor's funds, are utilized for the purchase of assets from a buyer to be used on a future date. The SPV provides the funds to the buyer and requires agent involvement in order to sell the future assets, since the investors will expect a return in money for their investment and not an actual asset. In a *salam*-based *ṣukūk* the proceeds from the sale, derived from the costs of the initial asset plus profit, are returned to the holder of the *ṣukūk*. Many companies use *salam ṣukūk* to fund short term liquidity and it is considered as one of the main eligible types of Shariah compliant *ṣukūk*.

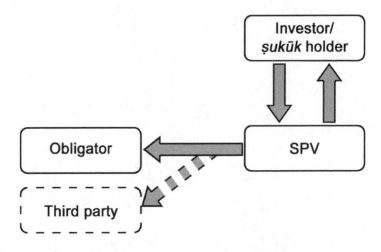

Figure 7.6: The *Salam Ṣukūk* Structure

7.3 Differences between Conventional Bonds and Islamic Bonds

Ṣukūk Islamic bonds differ considerably from the issuance of a conventional bond, which uses prohibited financial instruments such as *ribā* that do not comply with the principles of the Shariah. Contemporary issuances of *ṣukūk* emerged to offer an ethical alternative to conventional bonds in the global capital market, and its surge of issuances was heightened following the global economic crisis. In Islamic *ṣukūk*, investors are primarily interested in balancing their equity portfolios with products that can facilitate the balance in a Shariah compliant way. Conventional bonds, however, do not have any religious benchmark or regulations as to the financial instruments used in facilitating the issuance and therefore can use unethical methods of issuing bonds.

One of the main differences between *ṣukūk* and conventional bonds is the fact that *ṣukūk* involves asset-backed securities and not debt instruments. *Ṣukūk* predominantly represents the ownership of a tangible asset, project, investment, joint venture, usufruct of an asset or business, in contrast to conventional bonds that can be used as debt instruments. Unlike conventional bonds, *ṣukūk* does not derive any profit from *ribā* payments or transactions – due to the prohibition of *ribā* in adherence to the Shariah – and any investor who purchases a *ṣukūk* is rewarded a share of the profits that are derived from the asset.

Both conventional and *ṣukūk* Islamic bonds are issued with specified maturity dates, whereby the issuer buys the issuances back through an SPV. This type of initial investment does not give a guaranteed return of the principle amount invested into the project, business or asset. Therefore the holder of the *ṣukūk* may not get back the entire amount invested because according to the principles of *ṣukūk* all risks of the underlying asset have to be shared by two or more participating parties. Under a conventional bond issuance investors are not obliged to share any of the risks, and one party may lose out considerably and one may achieve profits. In the case of a project or investment in a business that does not perform well the investor of the *ṣukūk* will also have to share in the loss.

According to many Islamic scholars, the guarantee of repurchasing *ṣukūk* made through an agent or *ṣukūk* manager is impermissible under the rulings of the Shariah. Many experts in Islamic jurisprudence argue that *ṣukūk* issuances are generally better off being repurchased based on the net value of an underlying asset with a predetermined price between both parties in the initial stages of the *ṣukūk* purchase. There are many types of *ṣukūk* that are issued alongside repurchasing guarantees from agents, but these types of *ṣukūk* are generally not accepted by Shariah scholars unless they utilize the *ijārah ṣukūk* contract.

One of the key differences between a conventional bond issuance and *ṣukūk* is the ownership of assets. *Ṣukūk* enables investors to have partial ownership of an underlying asset, which the *ṣukūk* is based upon, unlike conventional bonds that do not enable the investor to have a share of ownership of the asset. Therefore, investors in conventional bonds will not be entitled to ownership of any project, business or joint venture in which they have invested. In addition, they have the obligation of debt that is transferred from the issuer to the holder of the bond. Another key difference between *ṣukūk* and conventional bonds are the criteria set out for investments. Conventional bonds can be used in financing any form of asset, investment project, and joint venture as long it complies with the legislation of the respective country that it is issued in. On the other hand, *ṣukūk* has to adhere to the principles of the Shariah for any type of investment project, business or asset made.

The units of issuance for both *ṣukūk* and conventional bonds are measured differently, as *ṣukūk* represents the share of the underlying asset whereas conventional bonds represent the share of debt. In addition, the price of issuance of a conventional bond varies according to its face value and compliance with the credit worthiness of an investor, whereas that of a *ṣukūk* bond is based upon the market value of the underlying asset. The rewards and risks involved in both conventional and *ṣukūk* Islamic bonds differ considerably. Conventional bond holders are eligible to receive fixed rate interest payments throughout the duration of the bond issuance, whereas *ṣukūk* holders receive their share in profit from the actual underlying asset, and also share out any losses between the parties involved. In conventional bonds, the maturity date determines an investor's guaranteed principal return. The effect in the cost pertaining to the underlying asset also differs between conventional bond issuances and *ṣukūk* issuances because holders of *ṣukūk* are affected by costs directly involved with the underlying assets and may be exposed to higher costs; in comparison to conventional bonds, whose holder relies upon how well the underlying asset performed in order to obtain the rewards from it.

The main differences between a conventional bond and *ṣukūk* are the absence of *ribā*, the underlying asset, which is normally an element that needs to exist in *ṣukūk*, and the sharing of risks between the investors participating in the *ṣukūk*. According to the issuances of *ṣukūk*, profits cannot be guaranteed to be fixed as they could vary due to the ethical principle of profit-and-loss sharing. In addition, Islamic *ṣukūk* cannot be transferred or used as shares, whereas conventional bonds can be converted into a share at any time. Islamic *ṣukūk* holders are entitled to ownership, and that is an eligibility given to all holders, so that they acquire either partial or whole ownership of a project, asset or rights. Conventional bond holders, however, have a different type of connection with their issuer and work on a lender–borrower mechanism, whereas the issuers in a *ṣukūk* state themselves to be the 'borrowers' in a conventional bond contract. Conventional bonds also provide bond issuers with a complete guarantee of capital and profits gained, though there may be interest involved in the financial contracts used within a conventional bond to facilitate the issuance. *Ṣukūk*, however, has no capital guarantee but a third party could voluntarily act as a guarantee or guarantor. The third party guarantee in the issuance of a *ṣukūk* Islamic bond will only work providing the guarantee contract is an individual contract between the two or more parties involved in the *ṣukūk*. This ensures that the guarantee is an independent contract between the parties involved in facilitating the *ṣukūk*.

	Ṣukūk	Conventional bonds
Asset ownership	• *Ṣukūk* give the investor partial ownership in the asset on which the *ṣukūk* is based.	• Bonds do not give the investor a share of ownership in the asset, project, business, or joint venture they support. They are a debt obligation from the issuer to the bond holder.
Investment criteria	• The asset on which *ṣukūk* is based must be Shariah compliant.	• Generally, bonds can be used to finance any asset, project, business, or joint venture that complies with the bond holder.
Issue unit	• Each *ṣukūk* represents a share of the underlying asset.	• Each bond represents a share of debt.
Issue price	• The face value of *ṣukūk* is based on the market value of the underlying asset.	• The face value of a bond price is based on the issuer's credit worthiness (including its rating).
Investment rewards and risk	• *Ṣukūk* holders receive a share of profits from the underlying asset (and accept a share of any loss incurred).	• Bond holders receive regularly scheduled (and often fixed rate) interest payments for the life of the bond, and their principal is guaranteed to be returned at the bond's maturity date.
Effects of costs	• *Ṣukūk* holders are affected by costs related to the underlying asset. Higher costs may translate to lower investor profits and vice versa.	• Bond holders generally aren't affected by costs related to the asset, project, business, or joint venture they support. The performance of the underlying asset doesn't affect investor rewards.

**Table 7.1: Summary of the Differences between
Conventional Bonds and *Ṣukūk***

Although the use of *ṣukūk* Islamic bonds are disputed by some Islamic scholars they can be used in a Shariah compliant manner if they adhere to certain conditions, such as the sharing of profit-and-loss and the existence of an underlying asset. This will ensure that the *ṣukūk* issuance can be Shariah compliant and used under a Shariah compliant contract such as the *ijārah* leasing contract. Conventional bonds continue to represent debt, and any form of debt that involves *ribā* is strictly prohibited under the Shariah and will generally not be accepted or classed as permissible under Islamic finance. Therefore, issuers and investors have to be aware of the key differences between *ṣukūk* and conventional bonds and structure the *ṣukūk* in a Shariah compliant manner.

The global appetite for *ṣukūk* is growing at an unprecedented rate and many conventional bond issuers are turning to *ṣukūk* due to the equity nature of the products that govern *ṣukūk*. It has becoming a driving force, with global financial centres expressing interest in establishing *ṣukūk* issuances in their respective countries. The equity nature of *ṣukūk* can only help reinforce the differences between it and conventional bonds, as *ṣukūk* is based upon the needs of the real economy and not the synthetic economy. In addition, *ṣukūk* is predominantly based upon profit-and-loss sharing and all parties involved, as with most Islamic financial instruments and transactions, share the risks.

7.4 Major *Ṣukūk* Issuances around the World

The *ṣukūk* industry has seen phenomenal growth, with issuances being facilitated in many global financial hubs, including interest from the west to pave the way for *ṣukūk* issuances outside the Muslim world. There have been some major *ṣukūk* deals since its early inception, and these have left their mark as issuances that have contributed to the popularity of this lucrative Islamic financial sector. Malaysia is unprecedented in releasing the highest number of ṣukūk issuances to date, with the GCC following in second.[3] There are a number of countries that have recently tapped into the ṣukūk arena such as the UK, Turkey, Egypt and Indonesia.

In 1990, Shell MDS launched its first ṣukūk in the Islamic financial hub of Malaysia, and this propelled the country toward further issuances that set the benchmark for the ṣukūk industry worldwide.[4] It was surprising for many that a non-Islamic company such as Shell MDS had utilized ṣukūk instead of conventional bonds to facilitate their issuance, and this further highlighted the benefits of ṣukūk bonds in comparison to conventional bonds. More countries began to consider the ṣukūk bond market and Indonesia, Pakistan, and Singapore followed suit with domestic issuances. Singapore, for example, launched a quasi-sovereign ṣukūk in June 2001, and a further issuance in 2009 was worth $200 million Singapore dollars.

Ṣukūk instruments are rapidly attracting attention from the west, and Germany launched the first ṣukūk in Europe in 2004, which was a major milestone in facilitating the issue of ṣukūks worldwide. Issued in the central German state of Saxony-Anhalt, the €100 million (US$123 million) quasi-government ṣukūk was structured under the ijārah contract. Germany had tapped into the Islamic finance industry and went on to invest in its real estate sector using Islamic financial instruments. In addition, France also tapped into the ṣukūk arena when the French halal food specialist, Bibars, issued a €500,000 investment in 2012 to finance the opening of their new restaurant in the heart of Paris. In 2014, the UK government issued a £200 million ṣukūk bond,

---

3. S. Jaffer, 'Sukuk: from a niche instrument to a global financial alternative', p. 87.
4. A. Alvi, *Sukuk Report: A Comprehensive Study of the Global Sukuk Market*, p. 7.

maturing on 22 July 2019, which was sold to investors based in the UK and in the major Islamic financial hubs around the world. The UK's first sovereign ṣukūk received very strong demand, with orders totalling around £2.3 billion, and allocations were made to a wide range of investors, including sovereign wealth funds, central banks and domestic and international financial institutions.

A special mention should be given to the notable ṣukūk issuance for investment in solar panels in the German energy resources sector launched by Legendre Patrimoine.[5] In addition, in November 2012 the state of Munich in Germany pioneered in an initiative to tap into the Euro ṣukūk market when a financial company, FWU, issued one of the largest German corporate ṣukūk worth €55 million. This unprecedented European ṣukūk used the ijārah sale and leasing structured contract to facilitate the ṣukūk, which was created for innovative computer software to be developed by the Munich-based FWU Group and used for Takāful services.

The Islamic financial hub of Malaysia, being the most important of all domestic issuers of ṣukūk, issued three of the largest ṣukūk within a domestic market to date and dominates much of the major ṣukūk issuances, attracting investors from all over the world. In 2013, ṣukūk issuances rose to above US$14 billion despite challenges in transparency and standardization. It was reported that the issuances of ṣukūk grew to US$26.6 billion worldwide in 2013.[6] There are still prevalent challenges, such as the need for liquidity in ṣukūk structures and tackling trading operations, in order for ṣukūk to further prosper in the future. Qatar is another major player in the ṣukūk market, with a significant contribution to global ṣukūk issuances. The largest

5. Jaffer, 'Sukuk', p. 87.
6. Ibid.

individual *ṣukūk* issuance was reported to be the Qatar Sovereign *ṣukūk* in 2014, which was estimated to be worth US$9.06 billion, and was seven times the size of the lucrative Malaysian *ṣukūk* called tranche 1, which was a sovereign *ṣukūk* under the *wakālah* structure. Qatar also issued the largest sovereign *ṣukūk* and the Almana *ṣukūk* in 2011 that further paved the way for their key place in the *ṣukūk* market.[7]

The *ṣukūk* market grew significantly in 2017, in comparison to recent years, as volatility heightened in the international bond markets and investors are seeing more opportunities for investments in Islamic-based *ṣukūk*. This is due to the growing concerns over monetary policies in the US, which is currently the largest issuer of conventional bonds. The international demand for *ṣukūk*, and utilization of financial instruments that comply with the Shariah, is growing at an unprecedented rate around the world and many conventional bond issuers are turning to *ṣukūk* due to the equity nature that govern them. It is becoming a driving force with worldwide financial capital centres expressing an interest in establishing their own *ṣukūk* issuances. This can only help embed *ṣukūk* in the 'real' economy, which continues to differentiate between conventional bonds and *ṣukūk*.

7. 'Bring on the bonds: more expected from the world's second-largest sukuk issuer', in *The Report: Qatar 2012*, Oxford Business Group, 2012. <https://oxfordbusinessgroup.com/analysis/bring-bonds-more-expected-world's-second-largest-sukuk-issuer>, accessed June 2018.

CHAPTER 8

Takāful Islamic Insurance

8.1 An Overview of *Takāful*

Takāful is a cooperative form of insurance that is founded on
the separation of funds and the operations of the shareholders,
thereby transferring ownership of the funds to the policyholders.
Takāful is based upon the principles of the Shariah, and promotes
the responsibility of cooperation and protection of one another
in order to reimburse an individual or company for a material
loss. It has been used as an alternative to conventional insurance
for people who wish to adhere to the principles of Islam and
utilizes a *Takāful* company or operator. Regular contributions are
made by the policyholder to the *Takāful* service and are managed
responsibly and according to the Shariah. The history of *Takāful*
dates back as early as 622 CE, and is based upon the fundamental
teachings of the Prophet Muhammad (peace be upon him) and
the Qur'an. The concept of *Takāful* was known as *'āqilah*,[1]

---

1.   M. Ayub, 'An Introduction to Takaful – An Alternative to Insurance', p. 2.

which was a system practiced in Arabia that promoted mutual cooperation between the Muslims of Makkah and Madinah and introduced the first concepts of Islamic insurance.

Islamic scholars and experts in Islamic jurisprudence have tried to implement the basics of *Takāful* based on the morals exhibited through the holy texts. Most Islamic scholars agree that *Takāful* could pave the way to promote and support mutual benefit based on the model of risk sharing and cooperation. There are various models of *Takāful* but it generally operates when an individual makes a payment to a *Takāful* fund in the form of participative contribution. For example, an individual would agree in a contract to become a participant contributing to mutually helping other participants in the contract. If any of the participants were to suffer from a loss, misfortune or die during the contract then you would contribute to cover the cost under the *Takāful* that was being paid into. The contributions made to the *Takāful* fund are considered to be donations, which promotes a mind-set of helping one another. At the end of the financial year, any cash surplus that has accumulated is paid in cash as dividends or distributions to the policyholders, and any claims made by the policyholders are reimbursed. This model of cooperation and mutual protection is one that is recognized by the laws of the Shariah. The underlying principles that govern the *Takāful* system can help to develop and promote the highly ethical principles of Shariah compliant financing. Unlike conventional financing, *Takāful* enables people to not only benefit themselves but also help others.

Inevitably, every individual is exposed to the possibility of undergoing a loss of some kind, such as theft, death, accidents, and loss of wealth, health or business. Muslims believe that these losses are already decreed from God and are written in their fate. However, in Islam Muslims are allowed to seek cover or protection to minimize potential losses if an unfortunate event was to occur. Therefore, the system of *Takāful* provides a Shariah compliant way to purchase a type of insurance cover to prevent against these matters, just as the conventional system offers commercial insurance. However, it is important to remember that *Takāful* insurance is based upon the religious principles of Islam whereas conventional insurance would not be permissible due to the charging of interest and other prohibited features such as gambling or uncertainty. To purchase a *Takāful* plan an individual would need to consult a *Takāful* operator, who will be responsible for managing the indemnity programme. The *Takāful* operator provides details of the terms and conditions, and any policies pertaining to the plan, and will ask the new policyholder to make the necessary vows of adherence to the *Takāful* plan. Once satisfied with the policies and terms and conditions, the policyholder can participate in their own *Takāful* plan according to one's individual requirements, e.g. motor insurance, travel insurance and so forth.

Takāful first originated within the ancient Arab tribes using the system of a pooled liability, which ensured that those who committed a crime against another were obliged by the law of the land to pay compensation to those they had harmed. In 1979, Sudan launched the first contemporary *Takāful* company[2] to provide Shariah compliant insurance services, and the Grand Council of Islamic Scholars of the Organization of the Islamic Conference (OIC) encouraged the use of Shariah compliant *Takāful* as an alternative to conventional insurance. The market has grown considerably over the last twenty-five years and currently there are over 130 *Takāful* operators and companies globally in both the Muslim world and the west.[3] As *Takāful* is based upon the ethical guidelines of the Shariah, key Islamic concepts of mutual protection are exhibited such as solidarity and risk sharing.

---

2.   PWC, 'Takaful: Growth Opportunities in a Dynamic Market', p. 2.
3.   Ibid., p. 3.

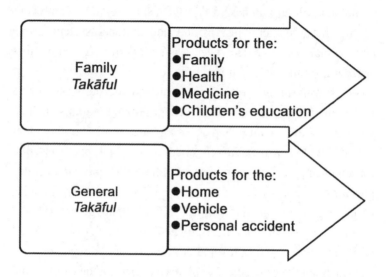

Figure 8.1: *Takāful* **Sectors for Insurance**

Takāful contributions made by clients are used in a pool system where small donations are made on a regular basis, either for general or family purposes. All *Takāful* companies are expected to operate under the principles of the Shariah and would need to consult an SSB in order to ensure that both the products and the operations of the company adhere to the principles of Islamic finance. In addition, *Takāful* insurers are required to invest in Shariah compliant products and services and to not make investments in anything that does not comply with the Shariah framework for *Takāful*. The ethical framework and transparency of *Takāful* has attracted both Muslims wishing to adhere to their faith in investing in insurance and also non-Muslims who appreciate the ethical principles of *Takāful*, such as the fact that no interest is involved. *Takāful* companies have to ensure the contributions made in the pool from policyholders share each other's liability, so that if one policyholder needs to be paid this is paid out of the pool of the contributions made by each policyholder. Overall, the key concepts of *Takāful* such as mutual protection, cooperation and solidarity make it a highly ethical alternative to conventional insurance and provides an ethical means of protection against unfortunate events.

8.2 The Principles of *Takāful*

Takāful is primarily based on the principles of Shariah, which had been prescribed to Muslims through the Qur'an and the sacred teachings of the Prophet Muhammad (peace be upon him). The main governing principles of *Takāful* are based upon cooperation, risk-sharing and mutual responsibility. The core values promoted through *Takāful* involve solidarity for one another and mutual protection among the groups of policyholders involved. Every participant that contributes to the *Takāful* fund pool should have these key principles in mind and make their contributions with the intention of not only securing their own protection but also helping others in times of need.

The principles of *Takāful* are based upon the concept of *tabarru*, which is the Arabic term for donation or gift, and promotes the values of supporting one another in difficult times or through unforeseen circumstances. These govern the way the models and various types of *Takāful* are utilized in adherence to the principles of the Shariah. Each model combines one or more of the underlying principles of *Takāful*, which are implemented in various ways. *Takāful* always has to contain cooperative risk sharing, mutual responsibility, protection and solidarity amongst all policyholders involved. This principle of cooperative risk sharing is extremely important, as through the use of donation it is designed to eliminate *ribā* and *gharar*. In addition, it addresses the issue of social responsibility and promotes solidarity and the innate need to care about others.

A participant in *Takāful* has to make a small contribution or donation into the pool of money, which will make the participant eligible to receive funds from that pool in the case of an unfortunate event. This ensures the element of risk sharing between the participants, unlike in conventional insurance where the risk is transferred from one party to another and all risk is placed upon the insurance company in exchange for the payment of an insurance premium. The principle of risk sharing enables all the risks to be shared among the participants, so if a participant suffers from an unfortunate event all the other members will contribute to help them and assist them financially. All *Takāful* participants cooperate and adhere to ethical Islamic principles of cooperative risk sharing, such as social responsibility and solidarity. *Takāful* insurance is viewed as an ongoing contribution or donation to keep the *Takāful* funds in the pool.

Another key principle of *Takāful* is mutual responsibility for each member of the pool, as each is contributing to the fund and is therefore undertaking the responsibility of assisting in the alleviation of a misfortune encountered by another member of the *Takāful* fund. Mutual responsibility in *Takāful* is taken seriously, as every member's risks become a responsibility for all participants. Similarly, mutual protection has to be implemented by all participating members of the *Takāful* fund pool, as each member is protecting the other against misfortune, loss or theft. The principle of mutual protection was derived as early as the time of the Prophet Muhammad (peace be upon him) and goes hand in hand with the principle of solidarity among all of the participants in the *Takāful* fund pool. Participants are not only concerned with their own protection against misfortune but also aid with helping others that suffer a misfortune in their lives.

Some of the other principles that govern *Takāful* are that policyholders must cooperate with one another and have each other's best interests at heart when contributing funds. In addition, any participant who makes a contribution should view it as a donation or gift to the fund pool, with the intention of helping someone in need when an unfortunate event occurs. Most *Takāful* operators will issue a subscription to the policyholder so that they are obliged to pay in order to help those in need. In addition, all losses incurred in the *Takāful* pool will be distributed between the fund members and the liability of those losses will be divided equally.

The underlying principles of *Takāful* are the concepts of cooperation and mutual insurance, whereby all participants agree to help one another by contributing to the fund and hold common purpose that in an unfortunate event or loss the donations they had made through the *Takāful* pool system will be of benefit. The Shariah compliant principles governing *Takāful* ensure that the participants' main interest is to fund the pool for one another, and with a socially responsible mind-set. Any participant adhering to the principles of *Takāful* is not allowed to make investments that involve any of the elements that constitute impermissibility.

The ethical principles of *Takāful*, such as cooperative risk sharing, solidarity, mutual protection and mutual responsibility, create the basis for a highly appealing and ethical system of protection against misfortune in a Shariah compliant manner. The majority of Islamic scholars accept these principles as the basis for making *Takāful* contributions, dating back to the times of the Prophet Muhammad (peace be upon him), and scholars particularly encourage the role of risk sharing and responsibility for one another. Some Muslims feel that there is no need to take out an insurance cover, as it is a duty upon a Muslim to help one another in times of need. However, due to global practices and the economic world, insurance and banking plays a pivotal role, and if executed in a Shariah compliant manner many Muslims feel that insurance can help in wavering and alleviating others hardship when a misfortune does occur.

8.3 The Main Models of *Takāful*

There are three main models of *Takāful*, and various other variations based on these three that have been developed, which include the *muḍārabah* model, based on profit sharing, the *wakālah* model, based on an agency fee, and the *waqf* model, where the contributed capital cannot be redeemed. The most important variation in all these three types of models is the combination of *muḍārabah* and *wakālah* to implement *Takāful* operations.

The *muḍārabah* model works when a participant and the operator enter into the *muḍārabah* contract. For *Takāful* this would mean entering into a contract of profit sharing between the *Takāful* participants and the operator. Under this arrangement, a profit sharing contract is signed between the operator, as the *muḍārib* who is responsible for managing the *Takāful* business, and the participant, as the provider of capital, called *rab al-māl*, who has the obligation to ensure that they pay the *Takāful* contribution as the capital. All profits are pre-defined in the contract of the *Takāful* business and the ratio to be shared between the two parties will be transparent. Any profits acquired in *Takāful* are defined as returns on the investment and surplus from the underwriting in relation to the *Takāful* funds only. Therefore, profits posted by the Shareholders' Fund are not included. Under the *muḍārabah* model, all profit sharing will be undertaken only after all the obligations of *Takāful* have been accounted for by the operator and *rab al-māl*. In the event of a loss or deficit of the *Takāful* fund, the loss will be for the participants of the *Takāful* fund.

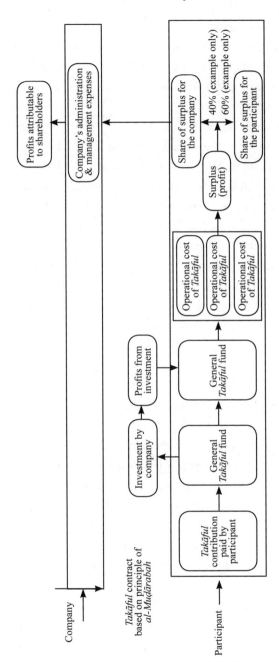

Figure 8.2: The *Muḍārabah Takāful* Model

The *wakālah* model for *Takāful* is based upon an agency fee, where the *Takāful* operator acts as the agent and works on behalf of the participants of the pool fund. Under this model, an agency relationship is implemented between the operator acting as a '*wakil*' to the participant. The operator earns a profit for any *Takāful*-related services given to the participants. Again, like the *muḍārabah* model a fixed predetermined fee can be stated in the contract or an agreed profit or surplus *Takāful* funds can be paid to the operator. In this sense, under the above model management expenditure can be charged to the *Takāful* fund as upfront charges. Under the *wakālah* model the operator earns revenue from the agency fee described in the contract, as well as returns on the investment of its shareholders' fund. If a cancellation was to occur, the participant will be refunded the net balance of his *Takāful* contribution, after deducting the upfront charges such the *wakālah* fees and any other expenses from the management of the fund.

The variation of this model developed predominantly in the Middle East is a combination of both *muḍārabah* and *wakālah* models, also known as a hybrid *Takāful* operation.

The *waqf* model involves making some of the *Takāful* contributions irredeemable to the participants who have invested in it. Under the *waqf* model the *Takāful* contract outlines the participants' consent to paying a contribution in return for participating in the *Takāful* product, which will be credited by the operator into the fund in accordance with the principle of *waqf*, or endowment. A *waqf* account has to be created by the operator within the *Takāful* fund to start the process. The operator will then utilize money as *waqf* to generate the desired *waqf* account. The *waqf* fund for *Takāful* is used to provide extended financial assistance to its participants at a time of loss and benefit its participants in accordance with the *waqf* deed.

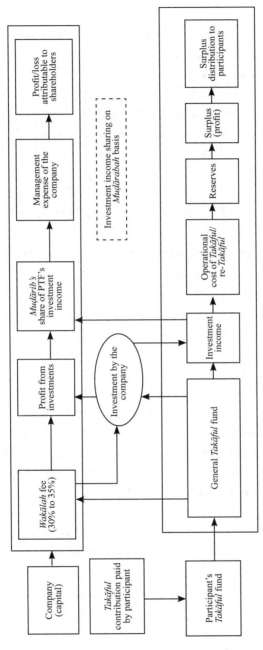

Figure 8.3: The *Wakālah Takāful* Model

Any expenses accumulated by the underwriting and operational cost of *Takāful* is normally charged to the *waqf* fund. The operator will carry out the necessary operations of the *waqf* against a *wakālah* fee, which will be taken from the participants' contribution to the *waqf* fund. In this model the operator will manage the investment of the *Takāful* fund including its *waqf* account, and its agreed portions of profits will be shared under the *muḍārabah* contract.

8.4 Comparing *Takāful* to Conventional Insurance

There are a number of significant differences between *Takāful* Islamic insurance and conventional insurance. Firstly, *Takāful* works in adherence to the principles of Islamic finance, which significantly sets *Takāful* and conventional insurance apart. *Takāful* companies not only adhere to the principles of Shariah but they also use distinctive features in their structure and operation.

Second, *Takāful* is based upon mutual cooperation between two parties, which means that all parties have to be liable for one another's losses in the case of an unfortunate event. *Takāful* is founded on mutuality, so that risks are shared by the participants who form a common pool. However, conventional insurance providers use a model of transferring risk from the policyholder to the insurance company with an insurance premium paid by the person being insured. Participants in a *Takāful* fund pool do not expect to make a profit from the pool and have the best interests of all participants involved, whereas conventional insurance is based solely on commercial factors.

Another key difference between *Takāful* and conventional insurance is that in adherence to the Shariah, there is no interest or gambling used in *Takāful*, whereas conventional insurance providers do include elements in which interest may be used and the contract may contain gambling methods. Conventional insurance has an increased level of uncertainty, whereas in *Takāful* the element of uncertainty is brought down to an acceptable level in accordance with the Shariah. This is because the contributions made by the participant in *Takāful* are considered to be conditional donations (*tabarru*), which are used for a good cause and to benefit other participants. The participants pay their contributions in good spirit, with feelings of brotherhood, and funds are only ever invested in non-interest bearing instruments. Conventional insurance, however, uses funds that are predominantly invested in fixed interest bearing instruments such as bonds and securities, which are strictly prohibited in Islamic finance. Any surplus accumulated from the *Takāful* fund belongs solely to the participants of the fund and is returned to them at the end of their specified accounting period. However, surplus in conventional insurance belongs to shareholders and the insured party is not entitled to any return on their payment contributions at any time.

Therefore, *Takāful* is an attractive option to those considering ethical insurance in comparison to its conventional counterpart. Conventional insurance companies do not have to abide by Islamic commercial law and can use many practices that are deemed as impermissible under Islamic finance. The nature of the *Takāful* fund pool and its operation is predominantly focused on the needs of the participant and the promotion of supporting one another in times of difficulty. This concept cannot be found in conventional insurance companies as they always benefit from a premium of capital paid to them.

In a *Takāful* fund, all the contributions are paid by the participant in the form of a gift or donation. Participants make these small contributions on a regular basis with the key intention of helping others in the *Takāful* fund pool and implementing mutual protection if a misfortune were to occur. However, in conventional insurance a premium is paid to an insurance company and the fee is earned by the insurance company in exchange for the premium paid. Therefore, all the risks are on one party instead of risk-sharing, which is distributed to all participants under the *Takāful* operation.

All *Takāful* companies have to abide by the rules and regulations set out by a SSB that approves the legitimacy of offered products. Conventional insurance companies are only subject to the laws of their own respective country. Participants who hold a *Takāful* fund account with a *Takāful* insurance company or Islamic bank can be reassured that the contributions they pay to the pool or account are separate from the shareholders' account. However, conventional insurance companies accept a premium, which is paid by a policyholder and is considered to be a form of profit for the conventional insurance company that can be disbursed to its shareholders.

In the event that there is a surplus in a *Takāful* fund the share of the surplus is distributed between the participants only, and any investment profits accumulated are distributed to the participants and shareholders through a *muḍārabah* or *wakālah* contract. Any surplus amount or profit involved in conventional insurance stays with the shareholders, and the policyholder does not receive any profit. In *Takāful*, the distribution of any profit is a fair and just method, in contrast to their conventional counterpart.

Another distinctive feature of *Takāful* is that the shareholders' capital is invested in investment funds which are wholly Shariah compliant. Conventional insurance companies utilize the capital of the premium, which is invested in financial instruments that do not adhere to the principles of Shariah. *Takāful* companies also have the distinctive feature of re-*Takāful* and their own specialist companies, whereas conventional insurance companies do not always have re-insurance options or specialized companies available that adhere to Islamic principles. There have been many

Islamic re-*Takāful* companies set up around the world to cater for Shariah compliant re-*Takāful* services and products. Islamic re-*Takāful* provides an alternative for participants to utilize in comparison to conventional re-insurance companies.

Having considered the differences between *Takāful* and conventional insurance it becomes evident that *Takāful* is based on providing for the benefit of others and not just one individual. *Takāful* promotes solidarity, mutual cooperation, mutual protection and the sharing of risk, whereas there is no moral concept to better the lives of participants in conventional insurance products. Conventional insurance companies use methods that transfer risk from one party to another, whereas *Takāful* enables participants to share their risk and promotes a sense of unity. In addition, conventional insurance companies do not share any surplus that may have accumulated through the insurance premiums paid to them, and therefore the participants are at risk of losing their money if no event arises where they have needed cover. Conventional insurance companies also operate with an eye to profit from their insurance services whereas *Takāful* insurance companies are based upon ethical principles which promote selfless giving with the view of also gaining mutual protection from all participants involved.

Therefore, *Takāful* could be considered as playing a more ethical role in providing services to its participants than just merely providing financial services to a customer. *Takāful* is wholly ethical in comparison to its conventional counterpart because every penny that is contributed to the fund is invested in trades that are both socially and environmentally friendly. Money is not invested in industries that harm society or abuse human rights but instead into highly beneficial causes and projects. There is a real need in conventional insurance to cater for the benefit and greater good of society at large, and this is exactly the need that *Takāful* fulfils. One could argue that conventional insurance helps individuals at a time in need, however, *Takāful* remains on a steady and ethical path while the conventional system is exposed to practices that may benefit only the insurer rather than the person being insured.

Takāful also promotes the spirit of Islamic economics that dates back to the times of the Prophet Muhammad (peace be upon him) and continues to provide a socially responsible, economically viable and ethical form of utilizing funds through *tabarru* donations. Unlike conventional insurance providers, *Takāful* providers enable participants to assist one another when a potential risk or unfortunate event becomes a reality, and this can hold social benefits and some level of financial comfort to alleviate some of the stress that a participant of the *Takāful* fund pool may be experiencing.

	Takāful	Conventional Insurance
Policy	• A co-operative policy where funds are contributed by donations from participants. The pooled funds can be used to protect other participants from risk.	• A policy that shifts the risk to the insurance company. An insured person pays a premium to receive coverage.
Buyers of insurance	• Anybody	• Anybody
Pooled funds invested	• Operators will only invest in Shariah compliant instruments which are free of gambling, usury and uncertainty.	• Insurance companies are free to invest in legal instruments like stocks, bonds, etc.
Profits (Surplus)	• It is shared among the participants and operators of a *Takāful* fund.	• Dividends are returned to shareholders.

Table 8.1: The Main differences between
***Takāful* and Conventional Insurance**

8.5 Growing Opportunities in the *Takāful* Industry

There are a diverse range of opportunities for the growth and progression of the *Takāful* industry worldwide, both in predominant Islamic countries and financial centres of the world. This growth has been achieved because of the ethical principles governing *Takāful* and its associated benefits to the participants involved. The market for *Takāful* is increasing exponentially with the rise of Islamic finance institutions through the demand for providers to cater for Muslims and ethical investors wishing to utilize Shariah compliant products, both for Muslims and non-Muslims alike. The industry is based upon the underlying principles of the Shariah and applies the key concepts that were established in Arabia at the time of the Prophet Muhammad (peace be upon him).

The growing *Takāful* industry provides for countries that have a large Muslim population, and those wishing to adhere to their faith, an ethical alternative to conventional insurance. There may be scope for the development of innovative Shariah compliant products, which are based on the ethical morals of Islam, to offer both general *Takāful* and family *Takāful* products. In addition, *Takāful* can provide options for medical and health related issues, accidents, education and mortgage life products.

Although *Takāful* currently represents a niche market in comparison to conventional insurance premiums, there is scope for the industry to further advance as the worldwide Islamic finance industry itself is growing at an unprecedented rate. Since its inception in 1979, the global *Takāful* industry has grown from a modest level of US$2.1 billion in 2006[4] to an estimated US$20 billion in 2017.[5] Major international banks and insurance

---

4.   PWC, 'Takaful', p. 8.
5.   B. D. Augustine, 'Africa, south-east Asia seen driving takaful growth' (*Gulf News*, 8 April 2018).

providers such as HSBC have launched *Takāful* units, which launched HSBC Amanah Takaful in Malaysia, to cater for the growing demand for Shariah compliant insurance products in the predominantly Muslim-populated country. There have also been many growth opportunities for the re-*Takāful* sector as the market continues to grow and develop in size. The challenge that the markets currently face are the need to offer Shariah compliant *Takāful* services that can outweigh the demand for conventional insurance products. In addition, *Takāful* providers need to meet the demands of the *Takāful* market and abide by the constraints and structures provided under Shariah law to be fully considered as a legitimate company. In order for the *Takāful* market to grow further, the treatment of taxes on family *Takāful* needs to have the edge over conventional insurance providers. *Takāful* and re-*Takāful*, which have been established predominantly in the Muslim world, are in need of investment capital and capacity to further develop their product offerings. If the *Takāful* industry has the right demand, and if participants view *Takāful* not only for its religious principles but also as an ethical alternative to conventional insurance, the market may expand further.

Significant investments in the *Takāful* industry can further expand the growth of the market, which has the potential to become a globally recognized insurance product. The *Takāful* market is increasingly concentrated in the predominant Muslim hubs of the Middle East and Malaysia, which has seen significant rates of growth for the industry at large. There are currently more than 300 *Takāful* companies around the world and more than half of these companies are situated in GCC countries such as the UAE, Saudi Arabia, Kuwait, Bahrain, Oman and Qatar.[6] The growth of the *Takāful* industry in the GCC is spearheading the market in comparison to conventional insurance in the same

---

6.   IFSB, *Islamic Financial Services Industry: Stability Report, 2017*, p. 28.

region. The *Takāful* market is expected to be worth over US$40 billion dollars over the next few years if it continues with the current growth rate.[7] Internationally based rating agencies have been eyeing the *Takāful* market and this can help in the capacity to build services to further progress the expansion of the industry.

The demand for *Takāful* products is based on the knowledge that its key principles are governed by the Shariah. If more people were educated in the benefits of *Takāful* in comparison to conventional insurance they may be more inclined to opt for *Takāful* insurance, as there are certainly more benefits for participants. In addition, *Takāful* is based on ethical and just methods, which ensure that everyone gains and benefits through mutual cooperation and protection. The industry has the potential to grow and if it tackles the challenges of gaining capital investment for the development of *Takāful* products and services it will more than likely see a further spur in growth around the world.

---

7.   Bank Negara Malaysia, *Takaful: Growing From Strength To Strength*, p. 1.

CHAPTER 9

Future Developments in Islamic Finance

9.1 Industry Developments

In recent years the Islamic finance and banking industry has grown exponentially, and significant events such as the global economic crisis of 2007 paved the way for the principles of Shariah compliant financing to be brought into the spotlight. Islamic finance and banking made its presence known internationally through the developments of Islamic banks and institutions that are rapidly emerging to cater for the demand for Shariah compliant products. One of the successes of the industry is its adherence to Islamic principles, which promotes growth, socially responsible investing and equitable risk sharing. The market is estimated to hold over US$2 trillion in global assets and this figure is set to rise as the industry grows.

The Islamic banking industry is expected to see developments in emerging economies such as Turkey and Indonesia that are implementing avenues to facilitate Islamic finance. In both these countries, Islamic intermediation and the increasing demand for

Islamic financial products and services has spurred the growth of Islamic banks and institutions. For example, in Turkey the government has turned its focus onto the Islamic finance sector and issued a *ṣukūk* worth US\$1.5 billion over a five-and-a-half year period.[1] In addition, Indonesia is also facilitating the development of Islamic banking and the sector is growing twice as fast as conventional banking in the country. By the year 2020, Indonesia expects to see one in five banks in the country as an Islamic Shariah compliant bank.[2] Africa is also developing its offerings for Shariah compliant products and services as the middle-class population increases. Countries in Central Asia and the Middle East have scope for developing the Islamic banking industry further, given the increased Muslim population and support from their respective governments.

One of the most notable industry developments in 2013 was from western major financial hubs such as the UK and France, as they realized the growth potential for Islamic finance. In October 2013, the British Prime Minister, David Cameron, announced plans to be the first ever western country outside of the Muslim world to issue a *ṣukūk* Islamic bond in 2014.[3] The *ṣukūk* industry is thriving globally, and the developments of issuances from both western and Islamic financial hubs in the Muslim world can only spur future growth of the industry. Malaysia continues to be at the number one spot for the *ṣukūk* industry and is helping to contribute to the growth in Islamic assets, which has been estimated as reaching US\$3.2 trillion by 2020.[4]

1. D. Tavan, 'Is Turkey Set to Embrace Islamic Finance?' (*The Banker*, 1 October 2013).
2. B. Ang, 'Indonesia Makes Progress in Islamic Finance' (*Investments and Pensions Europe*, September 2013).
3. N. Watt, 'David Cameron to unveil plans for £200m Islamic bond' (*The Guardian*, 29 October 2013).
4. Staff, 'Islamic finance assets forecast to be worth \$3.2trn by 2020' (*Arabian Business*, 7 August 2016).

Currently, the *Takāful* industry is highly concentrated in Malaysia and the GCC, although a number of emerging markets are developing to launch *Takāful* insurance in this niche sector. According to the ICD–Thomson Reuters *Islamic Finance Development Report 2018*, the top three countries which have made significant developments in all aspects of Islamic finance and banking were Malaysia, Bahrain and the UAE, establishing themselves as top Islamic financial hubs.[5] In addition, there were significant contributions to the development of Islamic finance and banking products and services in countries such as Qatar, Indonesia, Jordan and the UAE, among others who had significantly developed their Islamic finance sector. Development in areas such as governance, *Takāful*, *ṣukūk* and funds saw significant contributions from four GCC countries that made it to the top ten countries for development in the Islamic finance industry in 2017, the most recent year that figures were reported. There is room for development in areas such as *Takāful*, which is still relatively a niche sector in comparison to Islamic banking. Saudi Arabia is one of the largest providers of *Takāful* products and services to date, followed by Iran, with assets amounting to US\$15 billion and US\$12 billion, respectively.[6]

Non-Muslim regions such as the US and Europe have done relatively well in developing product offerings for the facilitation of *ṣukūk*. However, Malaysia continues to hold the top position for the number of issuances and its thriving *ṣukūk* sector attracts investors from around the world. Malaysia accounted for US\$204 billion of *ṣukūk* in 2017, followed by Saudi Arabia with US\$81 billion.[7] In addition, the developments of the scope for the Islamic investment sector have seen a significant growth with more

---

5.   S. Mohamed, A. Goni and S. Hasan, 'Islamic Finance Development Report 2018' (*ICD–Thomson Reuters*, 2018). p. 10.
6.   Ibid., p. 18.
7.   Ibid., p. 20.

countries investing in areas such as *ṣukūk* and Islamic banking products to fund their projects or investments in an ethical and socially responsible manner.

The advancement of the Islamic finance and banking industry and the growth of popular financial Islamic sectors such as *ṣukūk* and *Takāful* can further pave the way for more developments in the years to come. Many countries around the world are developing and facilitating improvements in legislation and services to cater for the growing demand for Shariah compliant finance and banking products. In order for the industry to further develop there is still the need for standardization of Shariah compliancy between SSBs in their respective countries. Standardization and harmonization, and a benchmark facilitated by Islamic scholars for deeming what financial instruments are Shariah compliant, can further help with the development of this rapidly growing industry. It can also aid in facilitating new product offerings and services that adhere to the principles of Islam, especially as the demand for Shariah compliant products grows worldwide.

9.2 Accounting Practices and Policy Developments in Islamic Banking

The accounting practices and policies used in Islamic financial institutions can vary considerably in financial reporting, and there is a need for standardization of the industry at large. This need has been emphasized with the growth of the global Islamic finance and banking industry and it is imperative that common accounting and auditing standards are agreed upon and implemented in all Islamic financial institutions.

The Accounting and Auditing Organization for Islamic Financial Institutions (AAOIFI) was established to cater for accounting and policy needs and was developed in the major

Islamic financial hub of Bahrain. AAOIFI has played a significant role in developing and promoting accounting standards and practices for Islamic finance and banking institutions and has brought together a governing Shariah Board, which works alongside Shariah regulatory and financial institutions to implement and develop its standards. The organizational structure of AAOIFI includes a general assembly and fifty-six institutions from fifteen countries and the AAOIFI has also issued eighteen pronouncements of standards to date.[8] The growth of the Islamic finance industry has placed increased pressure on the need for harmonization in determining Shariah compliancy through accounting and auditing practices. Accounting standards for financial reporting by an Islamic financial institution or bank may need to be further developed since some Islamic financial institutions experience challenges in accounting standards that differentiate from the principles of Shariah, as they were developed through conventional institutions that build their own product structures and practices and do not necessarily comply with the accounting procedures of Islamic financial transactions.

As the primary underlying principle for all Islamic financial transactions include the prohibition of *ribā*, the Islamic finance industry must adhere to this principle, and this puts them at greater pressure to enhance their practices. In addition, Islamic financial institutions need to improve Islamic financial risk management systems in order to benefit investors.

The Islamic Financial Services Board (IFSB) published a report in 2012 that demonstrated the developments needed to harmonize international regulatory standards for the implementation of Islamic capital products and services.[9] This was the first step

---

8.   R. A. Abdel-Karim, 'Accounting and Auditing Standards for Islamic Financial Institutions', p. 240.

9.   KPMG/ACCA, *Harmonising Financial Reporting of Islamic Standards* (London: Association of Chartered Certified Accountants, September 2010).

to paving the way for further standardized regulation, which addressed the challenges posed in developing accounting and auditing standards. Subsequently, the Association of Chartered Certified Accountants (ACCA) developed a report highlighting the need for the Islamic finance industry and the International Accounting Standards Board (IASB) to work alongside each other in developing the standards needed for investors.[10] ACCA also highlighted that additional disclosures were needed in order to facilitate Shariah compliant mechanisms effectively and the IASB would need to work with the Islamic finance industry regulators to develop harmonization of the industry's products and financial instruments used in Islamic banking and finance.

At present, the accounting policies adopted by Islamic financial institutions and banks are still in need of more standardized regulatory guidance, as some countries have Islamic financial products which are deemed impermissible and some do not accept certain products and services under the Shariah law. The differences in interpretation of what is deemed Shariah compliant in Islamic finance and banking can hinder the potential growth of development and progress of the industry.

One of the developments that AAOIFI exhibited in 2013 was the agreement with leading accounting firm Ernst & Young to develop certification of financial software for Islamic banking and finance products and core banking systems.[11] This was a major step in creating a benchmark for Shariah compliant financial software products and core banking systems, through the implementation of standards outlined by the AAOIFI itself. In addition, the development of the certification enabled AAOIFI standards to be implemented in Islamic financial products and systems. The AAOIFI has issued 100 standards to date through

10. Ibid., p. 4.
11. AAIOFI, 'AAOIFI and Ernst & Young to cooperate on Islamic core banking system certification' (AAIOFI, 2013).

Shariah compliant accounting and auditing, ethics and governance for the global Islamic financial industry and is making key progress in their attempt to harmonize Islamic finance practices around the world.

There are a number of key regulatory authorities that govern the industry, such as the IFSB, which can also help with the facilitation of standardization of accounting practices and policies – the primary challenge for the growing sector. IFSB aims to introduce new standards and cater for international standards that are compliant with the principles of the Shariah. The IFSB complements the work of the Basel Committee and is based in the Islamic financial hub of Kuala Lumpur, Malaysia. The accounting and policy developments from the AAOIFI and other Islamic financial regulatory bodies can aid in the progress of the Islamic finance and banking industry worldwide. Although there is a need for standardization it has not hindered the growth of Islamic finance sectors such as Islamic banking and *ṣukūk*, which is doing considerably well worldwide.

There have been challenges in implementing conventional accounting standards to Islamic standards for Islamic finance products and services, but this can be overcome with the establishment of harmonized Islamic accounting standards. The development of a new governance standard for the Shariah Supervisory Board commenced in January 2012 and the first tranche of standards were finalized in mid-2013. There are currently thirty-one accounting standards listed with the AAOIFI and these include frameworks for financial reporting, disclosures and investment standards covering a range of Islamic financial instruments, such as *muḍārabah*, *mushārakah*, *ijārah* and many others. There are five auditing standards, eight governance standards and two codes of ethics listed on the AAOIFI. The five auditing standards currently listed cover the objectives and principles of auditing, auditor's report, terms of audit engagement, testing for compliance with Shariah rules and principles by an external auditor and the auditor's responsibility to consider fraud and error in an audit of financial statements.[12] The development of future Islamic financial products and services may highlight the need for new standards to be developed to cater for the growing sector of Islamic finance and banking.

9.3 Challenges Facing Islamic Finance

As the Islamic finance and banking industry has grown to over US$2 trillion, there are inevitably more challenges that need to be addressed in catering for the rising demand of Shariah compliant products and services. Among these challenges are several opportunities for implementation of developments in Islamic financial services to cater for the world's rising Islamic population, which in turn promotes increasing demand in Islamic investments.

Islamic finance and banking not only appeals to Muslims wanting to utilize Shariah compliancy in managing their financing, but it also attracts ethical investors. However, due to the increased costs involved in facilitating Islamic financial developments and the lower returns in comparison to conventional financing there is room for improvement. Among the challenges that the Islamic finance and banking industry currently face there is a real need for trained experts in the industry from all levels, such as bankers, investors, customer service staff in Islamic banks and financial institutions and regulators. There is a real shortage of qualified human resource experts and Islamic financial professionals who can apply their knowledge in Islamic banking and finance.

---

12. AAIOFI, 'Standards Development and Revision Processes' (*AAIOFI*, undated).

Therefore, the Islamic finance industry needs to aid in utilizing funds for the relevant education and training of employers and employees working in the Islamic finance industry and Shariah compliant financial institutions. With significant educational training, the Islamic finance and banking industry can further progress and prosper in developing new products and services to cater for the growing industry. This can also improve customer relations between employers and staff and build a sound operational system when managing Islamic finance institutional practices.

In addition, the lack of Shariah scholars in Islamic finance presents with two main problems. One problem is the over-reliance on general Shariah scholars when advising on the implementation of Islamic financial instruments and transactions. Due to the global growth of the Islamic financial industry there are not enough scholars with knowledge of the industry to give guidance on what is deemed Shariah compliant and what is not. This therefore creates differences in interpretation of the Shariah, and what may be deemed Shariah compliant for one financial institution may not be permissible for another. Therefore, there needs to be improved development of standardization in determining Shariah compliancy and gaining guidance from scholars with a thorough knowledge of the Islamic finance sector.

The lack of standardization and harmonization of the industry has been a key challenge throughout the years, and this problem has been further heightened due to the expansion of Islamic financial institutions and banks around the world. In addition, many non-Muslim countries in the west are also tapping into the Islamic finance industry and may be unaware of the principles involved in Islamic finance. Hence there is a real need among Islamic regulatory and supervisory boards in their respective countries to implement a standardized benchmark that all financial institutions and banks can abide by. This can improve investors understanding of what products and services are permissible in Islamic finance and what is deemed impermissible under Shariah law. In addition, standardization can harmonize the industry as a whole, especially if all institutions adopt the same framework in compliance with the true principles of the Shariah. The Islamic banking industry, in particular, needs to focus its efforts in facilitating new product developments and produce new research in order to cater for the competitive global financial market and attract more investors and customers.

Solutions for the management of liquidity also need to be revised in order for Islamic financial institutions to manage liquidity in adherence to the Shariah. The absence of a separate legal and regulatory framework that caters specifically for the Islamic banking sector and Islamic financial institutions is still prevalent today and can help diversify the sector and set it apart from conventional financial institutions. The Islamic finance and banking industry is based upon ethical principles that promote socio-economic advancement, social responsibility and just practices based on the Qur'an and teachings of the Prophet Muhammad (peace be upon him), and Islamic finance is part of a Muslim's faith and is not merely confined to focusing on profits and gains, as the capitalist system promotes.

Islamic banking and finance has proved over time that it has the potential to become an alternative system to conventional banking. However, there is a need for dedicated research and support from government to develop a sound legal and regulatory framework for the Islamic financial industry. While interest-based banking that promotes a core set of values based on the capitalist system has taken hundreds of years to mature to the level where it is today, we cannot expect the same level of maturity from Islamic banking, when it still needs to meet the challenges that are prevalent. In order to develop the Islamic financial system and truly reflect on implementing the sacred principles of Islam, we need to address the challenges and de-link the Islamic finance industry as a separate mode of financing from conventional financing altogether.

9.4 The Future of a Growing Industry

The Islamic finance and banking industry is growing at an unprecedented rate and is expected to grow to US$3.2 trillion by 2020. The growth of the industry has shown that Islamic finance and conventional finance can coexist and that Shariah compliant principles governing Islamic finance can attract global western markets. The primary purpose of Islamic finance, as an industry, is to promote social justice and responsible management of wealth. Shariah compliancy in Islamic finance is fundamental to all Islamic financial institutions and banks and leaves scope for the industry to thrive, as more countries tap into ethical modes of financing.

The industry is poised for growth in the years to come and is constantly developing new products and services to cater for the growing demand for ethical financing that adheres to the principles of Islam. The global asset value is currently estimated to reach nearly US$4 trillion by the end of 2023, which is a staggering amount, and some experts project that the amount will surpass that figure in the future. Muslims wishing to use Islamic finance and banking in adherence to the principles of their faith ensures that the industry will always have demand for Shariah compliant products. The Muslim population is rising around the world, and is expected to account for more than a quarter of the world population by 2030. If the Muslim population utilizes Shariah compliant products in adherence to their faith instead of conventional products then the future of Islamic finance and banking looks promising.

Conventional financial products often contain impermissible features, such as charging interest, gambling or investments in industries which are unethical and unjust. People who do not want to fall heavily into debt through conventional finance or wish to choose ethical banking will inevitably turn to Islamic financial institutions. Even non-Muslim ethical investors have seen the benefits of Islamic finance and banking as an alternative to conventional financing, especially since the global economic crisis of the early twenty-first century. The capital markets have been unstable since 2007, when the crisis left many conventional banks and investors staggering in financial turmoil, and Islamic investments made through the ethical principles of Islamic finance, which include the main concepts such as no interest and the use of profit-and-loss sharing instruments, are an appealing option for investors.

Transparency is a key principle in Islamic finance and banking contracts and this reduces uncertainty, so all participants of a contract are fully aware before they sign. This is yet another advantage over conventional financing, as Islamic investment products often carry fewer risks in the long term. Islamic finance promotes socially responsible investing and it is a sector that is thriving, with investors seeking out Islamic fund managers.

The development of Islamic indexes to cater for *ṣukūk* on western indexes demonstrates further scope for progression, with many western countries expressing an interest in investing in Shariah compliant indexes. Dow Jones, Standard & Poors, FTSE and MSCI have all joined the Islamic indexes, resulting in more investors from the west taking notice of Islamic financial instruments. The *ṣukūk* market is thriving and is further expected to grow, with major financial markets expressing an interest in the lucrative alternative to conventional bonds. The UK government was the first western country to issue *ṣukūk* and the UK Islamic capital markets are showing considerable growth for the future.

Islamic financial hubs such as Malaysia continue to occupy the top spot for the *ṣukūk* industry and the developments of issuances from both western and Islamic financial hubs in the Muslim world can only spur future growth of the industry and help to contribute to the overall growth of Islamic assets.

The countries of the GCC excel in offering Shariah compliant financial products and services to a lucrative market and the UAE, Bahrain, Qatar and Oman are amongst the top ranking Islamic financial hubs of the world. Many investors are looking for stable and ethical investments that they can get involved in and Islamic financial investments can provide them with an alternative to conventional investments. The GCC is also a lucrative area for *Takāful*, with the estimated *Takāful* industry expected to rise to over US$40 billion over the next few years. The growth figures for many key Islamic financial sectors have exhibited resilience in the financial capital market. With an emphasis on risk-sharing and fulfilling socio-economic goals based upon the adherence to the Shariah, the ethical principles governing Islamic finance and banking show enormous potential for sustainable growth in the competitive financial sector.

As the Islamic finance and banking industry further evolves and develops to cater for the growing demand for Shariah compliant products, the industry has to address the key challenges such as standardization in order to sustain financial stability of the industry. The ethical risks and profit sharing models and instruments used in Islamic finance enable equity-based financing contracts that can support entrepreneurship and further enhance the scope for development of innovative and socially responsible investment projects. These projects can have a view to better the economic stability and benefit society at large so that it complies with the principles of the Shariah in promoting socio-economic betterment for all involved.

The future of Islamic finance and banking looks prosperous, as assets and key Islamic financial sectors are poised for growth. Islamic finance can only further aid in strengthening financial stability worldwide and promoting effective ways to manage finance. The highly ethical principles that govern all Islamic financial instruments, products and services, can further benefit the economic wellbeing of society at large, especially since most Islamic investments are socially responsible and many investors that utilize Shariah compliant instruments engage in beneficial projects such as infrastructure, medical projects, *Takāful*, educational development or charitable projects. The future of Islamic banking and finance is dependent upon the growing demand and adherence to the overall values promoted through *fiqh*, which is the Arabic term for Islamic jurisprudence. *Fiqh* plays a pivotal role in an individual's understanding of *maqāṣid al-Shariah*, which constitutes the higher ideals of Islamic law and governance.

Islamic finance and banking are not totally autonomous or self-contained and can be used as a stepping-stone towards the establishment of an Islamic economy, which affects all aspects of life. Islamic finance and banking has the potential to create a stable financial economy worldwide and promotes core ethical values such as socially responsible investing, mutual cooperation and protection, profit-and-loss sharing of risks and economic enhancement of society at large. The future of Islamic finance and banking can be lucrative in enhancing the economies of many countries around the world that are tapping into this growing sector.

Further Reading

Akkizidis, I. and S. Khandelwal, *Financial Risk Management for Islamic Banking and Finance* (London: Palgrave Macmillan, 2008).

Ali, R., *Sukuk and Islamic Capital Markets: A Practical Guide* (Winchester: Globe Law and Business, 2010).

Alvi, I. A., *IIFM Sukuk Report: A Comprehensive Study of the Global Sukuk Market*, first edition (International Islamic Financial Market, 2018).

Ayub, M., *Understanding Islamic Finance* (Chichester, Wiley Finance, 2007).

Banerjee, A., *Islamic Investments: Issues and Country Experiences* (New Delhi: SBS Publishers, 2009).

Kabir Hassan, M., R. N. Kayed and U. A. Oseni, *Introduction to Islamic Banking and Finance* (Harlow: Pearson Education Limited, 2013).

Iqbal, Z., 'Islamic Financial Systems', *Finance and Development* (June 1997), pp. 43–44. <http://www.imf.org/external/pubs/ft/fandd/1997/06/pdf/iqbal.pdf>, accessed June 2018.

Jaffer, S. (ed.), *Islamic Wealth Management: A Catalyst for Global Change and Innovation*, first edition (London: Euromoney Books, 2009).

Jaffer, S. (ed.), *Islamic Investment Banking: Emerging Trends, Developments and Opportunities*, first edition (London: Euromoney Books, 2010).

Jaffer, S., *Global Growth Opportunities and Challenges in the Sukuk Market* (London: Euromoney Publishers, 2011).

Mawdudi, S. A. A., *First Principles of Islamic Economics* (Markfield, Leicester: The Islamic Foundation, 2011).

Obaidullah, M., (2005) *Islamic Financial Services* (Jeddah, Saudi Arabia: Islamic Economics Research Center, King Abdulaziz University, 2005).

Wilson, R., 'Islamic Financial Instruments, *Arab Law Quarterly*, 6/2 (1991), pp. 205–214.

Glossary

AAIOFI: Accounting and Auditing Organization for Islamic Financial Institutions.

Allah: Muslims use the Arabic word Allah when referring to God.

Amānah: Refers to a deposit in a trust. *Amānah* in Islamic finance can be made as a transaction where one person holds funds or property.

Bay' bithaman 'ājil: A deferred payment or transaction made by a credit arrangement.

Bay' al-dayn: The sale of debt or debt instruments.

Bay' al-'inah: Refers to a double sale or deferred and cash sale between two parties.

Bay' muajjal: Refers to a credit sale and is a transaction that is often used by Islamic banks.

Fatwa: A ruling made by an Islamic scholar or expert to determine Shariah compliance.

Fiqh: Refers to Islamic jurisprudence and the principles of Islamic law.

Gharar: Refers to uncertainty or ambiguity in a contract or transaction.

Halal: Refers to something being permissible in Islam.

Ḥanafī: Scholarly school of thought in Islam.

Ḥanbalī: Scholarly school of thought in Islam.

Haram: Refers to something impermissible according to the principles of Islam.

Ijārah: Lease or leasing.

Ijārah ṣukūk: An Islamic bond that has the leasing structure of *ijārah*.

Ijārah wa iqtinā': A lease and purchase transaction.

Istiṣnā': Contract used to manufacture goods for purchase providing a facility for financing for construction of a project.

Ju'ālah: Rendering a service against a service fee.

Kifālah: A guarantee or assurance of providing.

Mālikī: Scholarly school of thought in Islam.

Maysir: Gambling or games of chance.

Mu'amālāt: All economic activities made by mankind.

Muḍārabah: A joint partnership between two parties; one who provides the expertise and the other who provides funds.

Muḍārib: The person who acts as an entrepreneur under the *muḍārabah* contract.

Muqāṣid al-Shariah: Arabic word for goals and purposes in Islam.

Murābaḥah: A sale purchase made on mutually agreed profits.

Mushārakah: An investment contract based on profit-and-loss sharing mechanism.

Mu'wada: A bilateral promise.

Qard al-ḥasan: A virtuous loan.

Rab al-māl: The person who invests capital under a *muḍārabah* contract.

Ribā: Usury or interest.

Salam: A forward sale transaction.

Shariah: Divine guidance from the Holy Qur'an.

Ṣukūk: An Islamic bond.

Tabarru: Act of charity or donation.

Takāful: An Arabic word meaning to 'guarantee' and is used in Islamic finance as Islamic insurance.

Tawarruq: Acquiring cash through trading activities.

Wa'd: A promise.

Wadī'ah: The trustee of a deposit.

Wakālah: A contract of agency.

Waqf: Religious endowment.

Zakat: The obligatory charity that Muslims have to pay.

Bibliography

AAIOFI, 'AAOIFI and Ernst & Young to cooperate on Islamic core banking system certification', *AAIOFI* [website], 2013. <https://www.thefreelibrary.com/AAOIFI+and+Ernst+%26+Young+to+cooperate+on+Islamic+core+banking+system...-a0319299818>, accessed April 2019..

AAOIFI, 'About AAOIFI', *AAIOFI; Accounting and Auditing Organisation for Islamic Financial Institutions* [website], undated. <http://aaoifi.com/about-aaoifi/?lang=en>, accessed June 2018.

AAIOFI, 'Standards Development and Revision Processes', *AAIOFI* [website], undated. <http://aaoifi.com/standards-development-and-revision-processes/?lang=en>, accessed June 2018.

Abdel-Karim, R. A., 'Accounting and Auditing Standards for Islamic Financial Institutions', in *Proceedings of the Second Harvard University Forum on Islamic Finance: Islamic Finance into the 21st Century* (Cambridge, MA: Center for Middle Eastern Studies, Harvard University, 1999), pp. 239–241.

Ahmad, A., 'Evolution of Islamic Banking', in K. Ahmad, K. Rahman, Z. A. Valie (eds), *Elimination of Riba from the Economy* (Islamabad: Institute of Policy Studies, 1994).

Ahmed. O., 'Islamic Investing: An Institutional Investors Perspective', in *Proceedings of the Fourth Harvard University Forum on Islamic Finance: 'Islamic Finance: The Task Ahead'* (Cambridge, MA: Center for Middle Eastern Studies, Harvard University, 2000), pp. 135–138.

Alasrag, H, 'Global financial crisis and Islamic finance' (Munich: Munich Personal RePEc Archive [website], April 2010). <https://mpra.ub.uni-muenchen.de/22167/1/MPRA_paper_22167.pdf>, accessed June 2018.

Alvi, I. A., *Sukuk Report: A Comprehensive Study of the Global Sukuk Market*, first edition (International Islamic Financial Market, 2010).

Ang, B., 'Indonesia Makes Progress in Islamic Finance', *Investments and Pensions Europe* [website], September 2013. <https://www.ipe.com/countries/asia/indonesia-makes-progress-in-islamic-finance/www.ipe.com/countries/asia/indonesia-makes-progress-in-islamic-finance/10003500.fullarticle>, accessed June 2018.

Anon, 'Takaful: Growth Opportunities in a Dynamic Market', *Price Waterhouse Coopers* [website], undated. <https://www.pwc.com/bm/en/services/assets/takaful_growth_opportunities.pdf>, accessed June 2018.

Augustine, B. D., 'Africa, south-east Asia seen driving takaful growth', *Gulf News* [website], 8 April 2018. <https://gulfnews.com/business/sectors/insurance/africa-south-east-asia-seen-driving-takaful-growth-1.2201789>, accessed June 2018.

Ayub, M., 'An Introduction to Takaful – An Alternative to Insurance', *State Bank of Pakistan* [website], undated. <http://www.sbp.org.pk/departments/ibd/Takaful.pdf>, accessed June 2018.

Bank Negara Malaysia, *Takaful: Growing From Strength To Strength*, (Kuala Lumpur: Malaysia International Islamic Financial Centre [website], 25 November 2015). <http://www.mifc.com/index.php?ch=28&pg=72&ac=154&bb=uploadpdf>, accessed June 2018.

Boerner, R., M. Gassner, and P. MacNamara, 'Wealth Management Cycle', in *Islamic Wealth Management Report 2010* (Dubai: Sarasin Alpen, 2010).

Dean, L. (ed.), 'Islamic Development Bank' in *The Middle East and North Africa, 2004* (London: Routledge, 2004).

Gafoor, A. L. M., *Interest Free Commercial Banking* (Groningen, Netherlands: Apptec Publications, 1995).

Hadžić, F, 'Conventional and Islamic Banking' (Sarajevo: Bosna Bank International, 2013).

Hanif, M., 'Differences and Similarities in Islamic and Conventional Banking', *International Journal of Business and Social Sciences* [website], 2/2 (2011). <http://www.ijbssnet.com/journals/Vol._2_No._2%3B_February_2011/20.pdf>, accessed June 2018.

IFSB, *Islamic Financial Services Industry: Stability Report, 2017*, (Kuala Lumpur: Islamic Financial Services Board [website], May 2017). <https://www.ifsb.org/docs/IFSB%20IFSI%20Stability%20Report%20 2017.pdf>, accessed June 2018.

Jaffer, S., 'Sukuk: from a niche instrument to a global financial alternative', *World Commerce Review* [website], June 2013, pp. 86–87. <http://www. worldcommercereview.com/publications/article_pdf/731>, accessed June 2018.

Jamaldeen, F., 'The Mudaraba Contract in Islamic Finance', in *Islamic Finance for Dummies* (Hoboken, NJ: John Wiley & Sons, Inc., 2012).

KPMG/ACCA, *Harmonising Financial Reporting of Islamic Standards* (London: Association of Chartered Certified Accountants [website], September 2010). <http://www.acca.org.uk/content/dam/acca/global/ PDF-technical/financial-reporting/tech-af-hfrif.pdf>, accessed June 2018.

Mohamed, S., A. Goni and S. Hasan, 'Islamic Finance Development Report 2017', *ICD-Thomson Reuters* [website], 2018). <https://repository.salaamgateway.com/images/iep/galleries/ documents/20181125124744259232831.pdf>, accessed April 2019.

Schoon, N, 'Islamic Finance - a history' (*Financial Services Review*, August 2008).

Staff, 'Islamic finance assets forecast to be worth $3.2trn by 2020', *Arabian Business* [website], 7 August 2016. <https://www.arabianbusiness.com/ islamic-finance-assets-forecast-be-worth-3-2trn-by-2020-641156.html>, accessed June 2018.

Tavan, D., 'Is Turkey Set to Embrace Islamic Finance?' *The Banker* [paywall], 1 October 2013. <http://www.thebanker.com/World/Is-Turkey-set-to-embrace-Islamic-finance>, accessed June 2018.

Usmani, M. I., 'Musharakah', in *Meezan Bank's Guide to Islamic Banking* (Karachi, Pakistan: Dar ul-Ishāt, 2002).

Watt, N., 'David Cameron to unveil plans for £200m Islamic bond', *The Guardian* [website], 29 October 2013. <https://www.theguardian.com/money/2013/oct/29/islamic-bond-david-cameron-treasury-plans>, accessed June 2018.

Wedderburn-Day, A. R., 'Sovereign SUKUK: Adaptation and Innovation', *Law and Contemporary Problems* [website], 73/4 (Fall 2010), pp. 325–333. <http://scholarship.law.duke.edu/cgi/viewcontent.cgi?article=1601&context=lcp>, accessed June 2018.

Wilson, R., *Development of Financial Instruments in an Islamic Framework* (Jeddah, Saudi Arabia: Islamic Research and Training Institute, 1991).

Youssef, M. B., 'Islamic Financial Contracts', *General Council for Islamic Banks and Islamic Institutions*, 2011.

Index